ABOUT THE AUTHOR

SHIRLEY MacLAINE, Oscar-, Emmy-, and Golden Globe-winning actress, has appeared in more than fifty films, been nominated for an Academy award six times, and received the Oscar for Best Actress in 1984. Most recently, Shirley was honoured with the 1999 Golden Bear Award for lifetime achievement at the Berlin International Film Festival and the 1998 Cecil B. DeMille Award for outstanding contribution to the entertainment field. She has also won two British Academy awards, two German Silver Bear and Golden Camera awards, two Volpi Cup awards at the Venice Film Festival, two Donatello awards in Italy and New York Film Critics and Los Angeles Film Critics awards. A longtime outspoken advocate for civil rights and liberties, Shirley is the author of eight international best-sellers – *Don't Fall Off the Mountain, You Can Get There from Here, Out on a Limb, Dancing in the Light, It's All in the Playing, Going Within, Dance While You Can* and *My Lucky Stars*. She lives in Malibu, California, and Abiquiu, New Mexico.

www.shirleymaclaine.com

The
Camino

A Journey of the Spirit

Shirley MacLaine

POCKET
BOOKS

LONDON • SYDNEY • NEW YORK • TOKYO • SINGAPORE • TORONTO

First published in the USA by Simon & Schuster Inc, 2000
First published in Great Britain by Simon & Schuster UK Ltd, 2000
This edition first published by Pocket Books, 2001
An imprint of Simon & Schuster UK Ltd
A CBS COMPANY

11

Simon & Schuster UK Ltd
1st Floor
222 Gray's Inn Road
London WC1X 8HB
www.simonandschuster.co.uk

Simon & Schuster Australia
Sydney

A CIP catalogue record for this book is available from the British Library

ISBN 978-0-7434-0921-6

Printed and bound by CPI Group (UK) Ltd, Croydon, CR0 4YY

For Kathleen

The
Camino

INTRODUCTION
The Journey Begins

Everyone holds his or her own philosophical and religious belief. Spirit is something else. By Spirit, I believe everything that we know and understand to be physically tangible and existent in the five dimensions is in fact the manifestation of a more subtle and nonvisible energy that exists simultaneously. Spirit vibrates at a higher frequency than the physical dimension and is the higher reality. Spirit manifests as life through form.

Thus I came to believe that the surface of the earth is the matter and form through which a higher subtle electromagnetic spiritual energy flows.

Just as human beings are the physical vehicles for expressing their spiritual and multidimensional selves, so the geological earth is the physical vehicle for manifestation of ancient memories and an alive inner Spirit.

Why, then, if Spirit flows through the earth and through all of us, is the state of the world so unfortunate? I couldn't comprehend the violence or, to use the old phrase, "man's inhumanity to man." The weather contributed to my confusion because it was obviously out of balance, which of course led me to conclude once again what I had learned years before from my spiritual and metaphysical studies—that nature itself is informed by the consciousness of mind. It was difficult for me, and almost everyone I knew, to keep centered and hopeful about where we were going as a human race.

Certainly Hollywood and the art industry I had been a part of all my life was reflecting values that, granted, might in turn be reflecting those of a great part of our society, but it seemed to me we were caught in an endless cycle in which we were witnessing the disintegration of decency, sensitivity, and the spiritual values that we as Americans had supposedly been raised with. What were we doing with ourselves? What were our human priorities? What did we wish for our futures and those of our children, and more than anything, why did we seem to so badly lack esteem in ourselves?

Now as a senior citizen, I found myself experiencing not only anger, loneliness, and anxiety over what we might be headed for, but fear that we were now almost completely out of touch with what we were intended to be in the first place.

I had a daughter, two grandchildren, a brother, and four nieces and nephews. My parents had crossed over, and I myself was contemplating how much longer I would have the physical life adventure on this world. However, I felt more creative than ever and had sufficient money, five or six really good friends with whom I could communicate on all levels (a rarity), a good healthy body, a sound mind (although some stand-up comics would dispute that), and a life that was "fancy free" and enviable to those who were tied down to existences of smothering responsibility. Sometimes, because of society's propaganda and conditioning, I thought I felt lonely, but when I gave it a second thought, I realized, with relief, that I was leading exactly the life I wanted to . . . unattached to a man-woman relationship, free of the rigors and restrictions of raising a family (husband included), unencumbered by a job I was not inspired by, and free to do whatever I wanted in the future. That was the question, however . . . what was the future?

Should I secure my roof because of the prophecies of high winds? Would there be a worldwide stock market crash? Would solar flares disrupt communications? Would there be one world government and buying and selling according to it? Would the viruses that seemed to be infecting humanity become more and more virulent because we were denuding the forests where they lived naturally? Would we become such a technologically addicted society that human appropriateness would suffer profoundly? Was our environment so compromised that it would never again sustain healthy human life? Were we alone in the universe? And if not, would they come to help us—or to finish us off? And was God out to lunch? Of course, I had more questions than even *I* could dream up. And, yes . . . I found myself at the point in my life where I had well-earned time to dream.

Perhaps it was because I was so free and open-minded that I had the time—and the energy—to contemplate what not only I but all of us were really doing with ourselves. My imagination could ripple back and forth across time until I found myself in a state of mind-time that provided some answers. But I am getting ahead of my story.

There is a famous pilgrimage that has been taken by people for centuries called the Santiago de Compostela Camino across northern Spain. It is said that the "Camino"—the road or the way—lies directly under the Milky Way and follows ley lines that reflect the energy from those star systems above it.

In Eastern philosophies the spiritual life force of the earth is called *prana*. This prana is inextricably linked with the life force of the sun, providing energy for all life.

The life force is especially strong along lines of energy called ley lines. These ley lines are the essential structure of the earth's etheric spirit. They are usually fairly straight, varying in width and intensity. A cross section of a ley line looks like an hourglass, the narrow middle intersecting at the earth's surface. The ley energy exists below the earth and above it, equally. This energy emanates at a very high frequency and, when experienced by a human consciousness, induces clarity of thought, experience, memory, and revelation.

The energy of the ley lines increases the rate of vibration of the etheric and dense matter that make up the human brain. The result of this stimulation is the production of more full, conscious awareness and information that was previously repressed.

This can be disturbing and frightening because it means that through this energy one becomes a more psychic being— for better or for worse.

The ley lines carry not only the spiritual energy of the earth in conjunction with the sun, but also the energies conjuncting with other galaxies and star systems.

The Camino, following earth's ley lines, begins in France, crosses the Pyrenees, and makes its way from east to west across northern Spain until it reaches an exquisite and very famous cathedral called Santiago de Compostela, where the remains of Saint James are said to be interred.

I have never been religious, opting instead to seek spirituality, so what interested me about the Camino was the energy of the ley lines themselves, as well as the challenge of walking alone for 800 kilometers (nearly 500 miles) and becoming essentially helpless and vulnerable along the way, as most pilgrimages require. The experience of complete surrender to God and self is the motivation behind most people's attempt at the Santiago de Compostela Camino.

The first inkling that I should do the Camino occurred in 1991 in Brazil. I was playing there with my one-woman show when my company manager, Michael Flowers, delivered a letter to me. It was written by hand and unsigned. Michael often sifts through my mail and, with an intuition remarkable to me, usually selects the pieces that he believes are important. Let me digress for a moment and tell you about his intuition. He has been with me as a company manager for nearly thirty years. I trust him, and when he believes that something that I haven't heard about is important, I listen. It is crucial to explain this, because he figures prominently in my story later on. I get all sorts of requests, and the most profound and craziest usually have to do with metaphysical, spiritual, and extraterrestrial matters. At another time, when I was performing in South Africa, he received a request from a mother and daughter who wanted to meet with me because they had had a close encounter of the third kind with space beings from the Pleiades. I met with the two. They seemed sane and logical, and when they finished the story of their encounter, I asked when they'd be meeting with their new space friends again. They said they were told the visitors would return when the pink house was painted white. They had not understood this remark until they told it to me, and this was the reason: My ranch house in New Mexico was in an isolated region where stories abound about spacecraft. It was pink when I bought it. But after renovation and considerable thought, I decided to paint it white! I have not yet seen their return, but it is something I'm haunted by.

In any case, the letter that Michael received when I was playing Brazil stated unequivocally that I should do the Santiago de Compostela Camino. As I said, it was unsigned. It was written in ink and implored me to do the Camino if I was indeed serious about my spiritual and metaphysical writings, teachings, and investigations. I was intrigued, thought about it, talked to some of my friends in Brazil who had made the journey, and ultimately forgot about it.

Three years later, performing again in Brazil, I received a letter in the same handwriting, again unsigned, stating that if I was to continue to write about spiritual growth, it was now imperative that I do the Camino.

My Brazilian friend Anna Strong agreed. She was a spiritual leader and counselor who conducted seminars in meditation and inner balancing. I respected her and knew that she had done the Camino and helped others do it as well. After informing me of what to expect and telling me that she would meet me in Madrid to help me launch myself, I canceled the summer movie I had planned and told my agent I was going to walk across Spain instead. He was used to my "reckless," adventurous ways, said I should get some good shoes, and adjusted to it. "Besides, you might get another good book out of it," he added.

Okay—fine.

* * *

The Santiago Camino has been traversed for thousands of years by saints, sinners, generals, misfits, kings, and queens. It is done with the intent to find one's deepest spiritual meaning and resolutions regarding conflicts in Self. The energy of the Camino was well known by people in ancient times to enable them more self-reflection and self-knowledge.

The history books trace the Camino back to Celtic times with the attendant mythological stories of cosmic revelations; multidimensional presences of gnomes, fairies, and trolls; and the aspect of its legend that interested me most—the fact that the trail ended in Finisterre, a few miles further west from Compostela on the Atlantic Ocean, which was thought to be the end of the then known world. I wondered what had been the previous unknown world. Was there a land that had existed prior to our recorded history? Was it calling to those of us who felt attracted to follow the Camino until we somehow touched it again? Why was the journey along the Camino supposed to provide the pilgrim with self-knowledge and an understanding of his or her destiny? There was almost a quality of urgency for me to travel it so that I could journey within the secrets of my own history—which harked back to a time longer ago than my imagination could conjure—almost a haunting knowingness that my personal reality would become more evident. But I was unprepared for the impact it would have on me.

It was—and *is*—my reality, which I am still adjusting to. My spirituality and the journey of my soul through time is the authentic discovery of my capacity to feel the alignment with the Divine. It is a theopathic state of consciousness. When the journey of the soul is recognized, a restabilization of the emotions takes place. There was no doubt that my emotions and the emotions of the world were out of balance when I began the Camino. During the journey I began to understand why. Many thought of the Camino as a religious trek. I could understand that because of the surrounding religious icons, churches, and reminders of what the church had established in relation to human life. But I saw how the church had attempted to mold its constituency into its societal perspective, sculpting the domain of feelings away from individual spirituality even as it claimed spiritual superiority. Then I realized that the world of religious domination of earlier times had given way to a scientific world today that sought to shed itself of the spiritual and emotional domination of the past in favor of a world of scientific, technological "facts."

Those scientists of human behavior who refused to observe through their own emotions were missing the point of reality. Individual feelings received no respect in their world. They had dehumanized human feelings and emotions, disregarding them in favor of what they term collective observations, which were agreed upon in the world. They didn't even give themselves permission to be human. If they were not rational and "scientific" in their observations, they were ostracized. Even the expression of emotion was unseemly in their world. Though they claimed to be seeking the truth about its inhabitants, in reality they were establishing a new mind-set that refused the capacity to feel.

So, in effect, science had freed itself from the domination of the church, only to become the modern dominator of the truth today. The chains have simply changed hands. The new enslaver of truth is science, and we are seeing its effect on human behavior everywhere. Without the recognition of the soul's journey within us, we are lost and only part of what we were intended to be.

I believe that the sorrow so much experienced in the world today can be regarded as the exercise of emptying ourselves of what went before, so as to make room for the joy that is rightfully ours in the future. We as humans have a moral obligation to seek joy. Then we will be in alignment with the Divine. But we need to acknowledge what has preceded our understanding of our lives, because therein lies the history of our conflict, loneliness, confusion, hatred, and separation from ourselves and God. If we can make peace with our ancient emotions, I believe we will have the capacity to live up to our moral obligation to seek joy.

On my journey westward along the Camino, I felt I was traveling backward in time to a place that began the experiences that made me and the human race what we have become today. Yes, I could say it was a mythological and imaginative experience, but then what is myth and what is imagination? All fancies of the consciousness are based on some kind of memory, or why would they be there?

1

Whenever I travel, I prefer to do it light; however, seven pounds of lightness was new to me. Having done the trek herself, my Brazilian friend Anna Strong warned me that each ounce I carried in my backpack would become tons after a few weeks. Sooo ... shoes would be essential and must be carefully selected— just one pair to walk in and one pair to put on at the end of each day. I have always had trouble with extraneous sounds while sleeping. I knew I would be sleeping in shelters *(refugios)* along the way with many others who snored, coughed, talked, and dreamed out loud. I wondered about my ever-present sound machine. Too heavy, I decided. I couldn't carry the batteries. I opted instead for earplugs, even though I had been told by my homeopath and acupuncturist that earplugs obstructed the meridians to the kidneys. I carried a light sleeping bag, two pairs of socks, two pairs of panties, two T-shirts, a small towel, a small washcloth, one bar of soap, one pair of shorts, one pair of light leggings to shield me from the sun's rays, some homeopathic remedies (for giardiases, nausea, cuts and bruises), Band-Aids, Nu Skin, adhesive tape, a water bottle (there would be fountains of clear water in every village along the way), my passport, several notebooks, a tiny address book, a few credit cards (which I vowed not to use), a little money (which I hoped I would not resort to), one Gortex jacket, one pair of Gortex slacks, one sweater (since I'd be walking in cold as well as hot weather), a sun hat, sunglasses, melatonin for sleep, and my precious Pearlcorder with many small tapes.

I am a Taurus, and therefore a person who accumulates things. I immediately understood this journey would be an examination of what was essential to me. "The road and her energy will provide all you need," Anna told me. "She will tell you what to throw away—and you will become humble as a result. You will see what a temple your body really is, that it is not a prison, and you will discover your essence." She told me I would find a stick to walk with. It would speak to me as though it would want to help. My feet would derive energy from the ground itself, which is why it is infinitely better to walk than to ride the Camino in a vehicle. I would receive messages from the path as though it was talking to me, until I became the path and all of its history.

I met with others who had taken the pilgrimage. They

advised me not to eat too much and to drink lots of water—at least two liters per day. There would be many good restaurants, but it was best to stay within the energy of the path's intent, which was to be essentially stripped of trappings. I should not be afraid of anything while trekking—first of all, they told me, the Spanish government protected all pilgrims and had harsh laws against interfering with a pilgrim's progress. I was told it would be better to walk alone, even though I would encounter many people along the way. Everything I carried with me would be a distraction. I should learn to let go. And I should be prepared to die, because to do such a pilgrimage meant I was ready to give up the old values that conflicted my life.

I could honestly say that I had no problem with dying if that was what was meant to be. I had had enough of the state of affairs as I knew them to be. I was ready for a new understanding to propel me forward for the rest of my life.

*   *   *

In preparing for my walk, I decided to rehearse with my backpack.

I packed all the items and one day decided to walk the hills of Calabasas in California as a precursor. That is exactly what happened. I felt "precursed" with what I experienced.

It was a trail I had often taken. As I parked my car at the entrance, out of the corner of my eye I noticed a Latino man, scruffy, no shoes, and slightly wild-eyed, in the trees near the trail.

I ignored him, locked my car, strapped on my backpack, and began my hike. I fingered my Swiss Army knife and made a mental note that I was safe with it. I also noted that I would try to make it way up the trail to a bench where I knew I could remove my backpack and rest.

Thus began my contemplation on how goal-oriented I was. A goal was so important to me that sometimes the reaching of it justified the means by which I accomplished it. I walked for miles thinking about reaching that bench. Then I walked even further. The backpack was heavy and the hike was becoming a struggle. I stopped and put some Emergency C into my water bottle. I drank and walked on. Finally, I stopped, exhausted, and realized I had long since passed the bench that had been my goal! The significance of this small event was not lost on me. I was truly disappointed in my overachievement. But I had often done such things, remaining separated from the path I was on because of my intense desire to reach the goal. Maybe that was the definition of "success" in this world. I was an example of the accepted term, when what I was looking for was the true meaning of "success." One has to achieve some version of success in order to know there is another version.

In any case, I turned around, retraced my steps, and after some miles, recognized the bench. I decided not to rest on it and continued down the mountain. When I reached my car, there was the Latino man, looking in worse shape than before.

"May I help you?" I asked him.

"My feet are burning from no shoes," he said. "I need a ride to my car."

I realized I was talking to a man of Spanish descent and feeling almost as though I were living a future event on the Camino. I thought, "I should be kind to strangers."

I offered him a ride to his car, which I supposed wasn't far away. He climbed in beside me. He was filthy and smelled bad.

"I don't know why I'm doing this," he said in a confused state.

"Sometimes we all do things for reasons we don't understand," I answered, thinking of what I would be doing in a week without understanding it either. I started the car and told him I was going to do the Santiago de Compostela pilgrimage. He seemed to understand and know it.

"Are you Catholic?" I asked.

He nodded and said, "Yes."

"Are you doing penance?" I asked. He nodded.

"Are you doing penance?" he asked.

I said I didn't think so.

Then he looked at my breasts. I had made a conscious decision not to wear a bra on the Camino because the straps hurt my shoulders with the backpack. It had occurred to me that such an elimination of underwear would be provocative. I wondered if I had manifested my concern into a reality.

The man continued to stare at my breasts. Oh, God, I thought. This could be dangerous. There was no one in sight for miles.

He finally took his eyes off my anatomy and said, "Can I make love to you?"

It was surreal. I slammed on the brakes and erupted. "Are you out of your mind?" I screamed. "What the hell do you think you're doing? Of course not, you idiot. I picked you up because you needed help, your feet were burning, you needed water and to return to your car, and this is what you do? You are outrageous!" I was furious, which seemed to activate some sense of misplaced justice in his mind.

"There you go, you see?" he said. "I *asked* you, instead of *demanding,* and you won't do it."

My mouth fell open. I was in trouble now. I thought of really going after him more irately, but something I saw flicker across his face stopped me. He had not touched me or advanced toward me physically. Then he said, "I passed my car. Let me out," he demanded.

There was no car in sight anywhere.

"Sure," I answered. He opened the door on his side and climbed out.

"Listen," I said, "you should watch that sex stuff, you know. It can get you in a lot of trouble."

Over his shoulder he said, "Yes, thank you. I know. I'm always doing this."

Then he walked away.

I sat in my car in a state of bewilderment. Had he been real? It was as though an experiential vision had just happened to me.

I turned to look at him again. He had disappeared. There was no man and no car. I vowed to never be afraid of going braless again, and I knew I would have to give much thought to the truth that reality was where the mind was *and* that I had been so determined to make a goal of my bench that I had passed it. . . . Reality simply was where the mind was. I could understand more deeply why I was an actress. I could manifest what I needed in reality. I had manifested a barefoot, filthy wanderer to warn me that the Camino was feminine and, as a result, human sexuality would rise. Everyone had told me that the Camino offered those who walked it a love affair. It was the individual's choice whether to take it. Some weeks later, I would be faced with that choice.

2

Most of us have a friend who has a soul meaning for us . . . someone (if we're lucky) to whom we can talk about anything. Kathleen Tynan was one of those friends to me. She was highly intelligent, but that didn't detract from her capacity to have a good time. She was a social animal and enjoyed the trappings of restaurants, parties, and good conversation. English, intellectual, and a great beauty, Kathleen did not fully share my spiritual interests. She was curious, I would say, but frankly tried to dissuade me from publishing any material that took me down the metaphysical path. She thought it was essentially wacky and would become a "career buster" if I shared my beliefs with the public. However, when she saw that, aside from some jokes, nothing like that happened, she became more comfortable with my search. She was also an extremely honest friend to me. Her deceased husband, Kenneth Tynan, the noted English writer and critic, had been a close friend too.

Kathleen continued to wear her wedding ring after Ken's death, even though she was involved with other men. Ken had been her anchor, her muse, and the man who was the link to (or substitute for) her father. She seemed to be using the men in her life to reach the true meaning of who her father had been to her.

When she visited me in Malibu, staying (to my delight) for months at a time, I noticed an ambivalence about the way she gazed out to sea, staring for hours and hours at a time at the water and sky in what seemed to be a confused yet resigned contemplation. I wondered if she was finally meditating about the unacknowledged spirituality in life. I came to understand it was much more than that. Kathleen was dying of colon cancer, and she knew it. Her doctors could find nothing wrong, but she insisted there was something there. Finally, with an MRI, she was proven right. They were stunned at the avocado size of the hidden tumor.

I've always wondered about Kathleen's way of dying. For years she had been expressing a profound desire to know her father more, who had died when she was in her teens. In the last years of her life, before she developed cancer, she dug out articles he had written (he had been a foreign correspondent), looked through family records, interviewed people who had known him, and searched her own childhood memories for clues as to his real identity, not only his personality and character, but his relationship with her mother, with whom Kathleen herself had had an arm's-length relationship.

She admitted to me that the men in her life had been roads to her father, but now she seemed compelled to know him again. I put my observations in a compartment in my mind until I learned about her cancer. I wondered if the disease was not the quickest way for her to reunite with the man she loved and missed the most.

When I called her in London and told her I was going to do the Santiago pilgrimage, she knew exactly what I meant because she and Ken and her children had driven it a few years before. "As a matter of fact," she said, "that was the last trip we took together, as well as a reconciliation. Ken was hooked up to an oxygen tank in the car"—he was dying of emphysema— "smoking and laughing with the kids in the back, as I drove, attempting to figure out what life was or wasn't all about."

She said traveling the Camino, even though by car, had been the pinnacle of their relationship, and on July 26, one year to the day after the end of the trip, Ken died. She was thrilled I was doing it and longed to see me in London before I went on to Spain.

"The cancer has metastasized to my bones," she said. "So soon would be good." Kathleen's humor about Ken's death and her own situation was breathtakingly English.

I said good-bye to my friends in California, most of whom cried when I left. I had taken many trips and said good-bye many times, but this occasion was different. They knew the dangers, I suppose, but beyond that they must have sensed something more. My friend Anne Marie told me to take forty days because it was the amount of time Jesus and various saints had taken in the wilderness. The people who worked for me (also friends) didn't really understand why I was putting myself in danger. My daughter and my brother, used to my wanderings, were detached and said, "Have a good time." My friend Bella Abzug thought it was another crazy, madcap spiritual adventure, which she couldn't really be bothered with, and two other close friends went to my place in New Mexico to hold down the energy there. (They both had Indian blood coursing through their veins and understood that land energy mattered in terms of balancing, even though I would be on the other side of the world.) The woman who worked for me as a housekeeper took me to the airport. We hugged, she cried, and I thanked her for being such an understanding wife.

* * *

When I arrived at Kathleen's place in London, I was shocked at her appearance and how advanced her illness was. She, however, was deeply engrossed in writing her second book on Ken, a volume compiling his letters and notes, which she had dutifully kept in filing cabinets for years. A word about Kathleen's fortitude: She was a beauty of such exquisite proportions that the incandescence of it blinded the observer to the suffering that lay underneath. She put my American "heart on my sleeve" honesty to shame. She was layered like a rose with each petal revealed, more interesting. Perhaps our identification with each other was based on something more basic: we were both Canadian. My mother had been Canadian, and Kathleen had been born in Canada, though she had long lived in England and had adapted to English ways and discipline.

Her discipline, even in suffering, was extraordinary. She wanted to attend a book party in London given by the publisher Lord Weidenfeld. She could barely dress herself or even walk, but she was determined to dispel the rumors that she was ill. I helped her dress and make up; we got a car. I was sworn to secrecy, and my task for the evening was to get out the word that Kathleen was in good health. My memory singes with the images of Kathleen holding court on a brocade sofa, her gray-colored cape covering her rail-thin body, her hair, newly coifed, spilling around her face (she never lost her hair during chemotherapy). She was magnificent. No one suspected that she had a tube in her stomach that emptied feces from her bowels into a bag hidden under her clothing, or a catheter in her chest that dispensed chemotherapy at different intervals. Even I was not allowed to observe these fundamental sufferings of her condition.

Of course the subtly swarming English social gossips did their number, asking me pointed questions and fawning over Kathleen after I explained she had simply had a touch of pneumonia, which was what precipitated the cancer gossip, for God's sake.

Lord Weidenfeld went around suggesting that "whoever" should write their memoirs. Kathleen's friends, with whom she had had only telephone contact, seemed satisfied that she was only tired from the pneumonia and went about exchanging the latest political gossip. Kathleen knew her constituency. She had accomplished her social task.

When I saw her slightly falter under the cape, I knew that she needed to go. Her courageous performance must not be betrayed.

We departed. She sighed and fell asleep in the car. I wondered if she would die while I was walking in Spain.

*　　*　　*

I stayed with Kathleen for three days. I spoke with her doctors, who were not hopeful; her children, who both had stiff upper lips; her mother, who was a steamroller of hidden judgments; two men who were in love with her, but didn't really understand what was going on; and of course, Kathleen herself. Our conversations were painful and profound. She had been given a few months, she thought, and wondered aloud if I believed she would really reunite with her father. That led to spiritual discussions that, when so personal, became difficult even for me. Let it suffice to say that she went through attempting to understand Ken's death from emphysema while remaining a heavy smoker. "He didn't want to die," she insisted. "He fought so hard to stay alive." I was perplexed in the extreme, but found it too painful to contradict her, for to do so would have been to raise the issue of her own impending death and her hidden desire to be with Ken and thus, beyond Ken, with her father. She was of the opinion that paradise had been lost on this earth and believed that the mystery of why that was true should remain a mystery.

As the third day ended, she asked me to call her from Spain when I had commenced my trek alone. She said she would then remove her wedding ring and wanted me to do the Camino for her. She reminisced about the Spanish countryside, the sunsets, the food, the religious meanings, and said she would wait for me to return and report on my adventure.

3

I left London with Kathleen in my heart and the need to have some time to contemplate the meaning of friendship and loss.

In Madrid I met Anna Strong, who had come to help me get started, as she had promised. She was full of anticipation about the walk and said she would start me off and then was going to leave to attend a seminar in Ireland.

We compared the weight of our backpacks, discussed essentials, and she handed me a Bible. "You must allow random openings," she said, "and read the page that comes up. Your higher self will give you what you need."

We stayed overnight in Madrid with friends of Anna's. It was to be the last night in a real bed, in a real house, with real hot water, a toilet with privacy, and quiet surroundings while sleeping.

We left for Pamplona the next day. We took a cab to Saint-Jean-Pied-de-Port, backtracking to France over the Pyrenees to the beginning of the journey. The curving road that we would retrace on foot careened over the mountains, and I got sick in the car. A good beginning, I thought. Walking would be a cinch.

Arriving in Saint-Jean-Pied-de-Port, Anna said we needed to visit a Mme. de Brill in order to collect our *carnés,* folded pamphlets that were the certificates of travel. The *carnés,* when stamped in each village, would prove that we had made the journey.

Saint-Jean-Pied-de-Port was ancient, cluttered with quaint red-roofed houses painted in white. Everything was closed, and the town was cold and dark. The cabdriver let us off at the Church of Notre Dame in the old section of the town. We crossed the river Nive, went down the rue d'Espagne, and through the walled *haute ville* by the Porte d'Espagne. No one was out in the evening, and Anna couldn't remember where Mme. de Brill lived. Thus I began thirty days of always looking for something I couldn't find. After knocking on many doors, some of which were gently closed in our faces, I found myself walking up some stone steps and down a dark hallway just adjacent to an ominous-looking *refugio* where pilgrims from Paris who were already on the Camino slept.

We encountered several disgruntled pilgrims in the hallway who rolled their eyes in disgust, having just dealt with Mme. de Brill. Apparently, she was famous for being unpleasant, and we were next on her list.

We knocked on her door. She answered. *"Mon Dieu!"* she screamed, then went on to say in French that she was sick with the grippe and tired. Her small television set was on, and an American military choir was singing "Mine eyes have seen the glory of the coming of the Lord." I would need that, I thought. A small dog barked beside a dog dish containing no food. Mme. de Brill was about five feet four, had uncombed gray hair, and was indeed a vindictive-acting, terrible person who would test one's spiritual patience.

She proceeded to make fun of Anna's sneakers, which were nothing out of the ordinary. Said sarcastically that we would never complete the Camino. Said she had never made the trek and didn't intend to, and after more dark-spirited put-downs, finally presented us with our stamped *carnés* and literally shoved us out the door.

Anna and I promptly found a five-star chalet restaurant and had wine and a delicious dinner, contemplating the contradiction between our proposed trek of poverty and our stations in life. Why not? Queen Isabella, King Ferdinand, as well as many other lesser known kings and queens had walked this contradiction themselves. Yes, even crowned heads had a need for spiritual wealth too.

After dinner we went out to look for the yellow arrows
that Anna said would lead our way. They were invisible in the
dark. I couldn't read any of the signs in Spanish or in French
and felt myself becoming more dependent on Anna than I
wanted to be. Would I be able to walk with others and still stay
independent? It had been an inquiry I had made early in my
life. I still was not sure of the answer.

4

I began the trek the next morning, on June 4, outfitted with my seven-pound harness on my back. The early morning was glorious with sunshine, and now I could see the yellow arrows that guided us out of town. I spotted other pilgrims ahead. Some walked in pairs; others were alone. There was no formal procession of pilgrims. They simply dotted the countryside and up into the Pyrenees. Most wore the scallop shell—the symbol of Saint James, which was the insignia of the Santiago pilgrim—on the back of their backpacks. I thought as I walked of those who had gone before me. The pilgrimages to Compostela had brought together a cross section of human beings from all over Europe. You could say that the Camino had been the legacy of medieval Christianity attempting to unite, through faith and devotion, many aspects of society involved with art, religion, economics, and cultural pursuits. People from lowly stations and saints and royalty disregarded their social distinctions and national borders in order to worship and find the divine in themselves on the journey to Santiago de Compostela. Together with Rome and Jerusalem, the Camino was the center of Christianity and all that that implied.

A bishop of Le Puy, in France, accompanied by a retinue of many followers, had been one of the earliest to make the pilgrimage in the year 950 and record it. Though the route was said to have been the scene of pilgrimages thousands of years before, no records of these earlier journeys have been found. As each century unfolded, the number of pilgrims increased, marked by the recorded accounts of their experiences. In those days people walked in groups for protection because bandits, thieves, and vagabonds were a source of real concern. The Knights Templar was a society formed to protect the pilgrims to ensure their journey of devotion. The churches and *refugios* along the way were offered as places of shelter and lodging, advice and help. Of real interest to me was the role of the Arab-Moorish invaders along the Camino in relation to the Christian world. I was struck by how similar were our conflicts today. To the Arab, the Christian was an infidel and a partner of Satan. To the Christian, the Arab was a heathen and ruled by the sword. Nothing much had changed. I didn't fully understand either point of view and would soon begin to see where my confusion originated.

Leaving Saint-Jean-Pied-de-Port was a baptism of fire—straight up and into the Pyrenees. I wasn't used to the lack of oxygen, nor had I established my pace. I could see that Anna was going to walk more slowly than I, and I didn't want to get too far ahead for fear of losing sight of her and making a wrong turn. I slowed down. I remembered how hard it had been for me as a professional dancer to take a slower beginner's class rather than a razzle-dazzle advanced one. The moves were more intense, more concentrated, and more painful because I had already learned how to bypass the effort. The same applied here.

We walked straight up for about five and a half kilometers (nearly three and a half miles), surrounded by hazel, chestnut, and white beech trees. Even in my breath-deprived state I was happy. The mountains were extraordinary. Cowbells rang out, their music dancing through the trees. From travelers far away conversations echoed in Danish, French, Spanish, and German. Along the path were the yellow arrows, sometimes crudely painted on the grass and rocks. Daffodils, buttercups, and purple flowers hugged the trees. I thought of my childhood and remembered the day I had walked to school and encountered an exquisite cluster of flowers. I stopped to gaze at their beauty, and I remembered being totally lost in happiness at that moment. I actually felt I had melded into the flowers until I *became* them. I *became* the consciousness of the flowers, with none of the earthly concerns attending a six-year-old. That moment has stayed with me always as an example of what consciousness in adult life could be if I allowed it. It spoke to what I had learned: that we are all part of everything and vice versa. What was blocking us from reverting to that truth whenever we needed to? And were we meant to be living in that state of mind, body, and spirit during the entirety of our lives? Why did we accept suffering as a standard-bearer of our existence? It seemed that all earthly religions taught that suffering was the natural state of mankind.

Just as I thought that, I realized a blister was developing on my right foot. I stopped. So soon? This was happening so soon? I had rubbed my feet with Vaseline, and my shoes were what I thought were a good fit. I sat down, removed my backpack, took off my shoe and sock, and remembered the same kind of blisters I used to get in ballet class. I promptly applied adhesive tape directly to my skin so it wouldn't rub anymore and prayed.

I felt a slight shiver up and down my spine, and then a presence seemed to surround me. I recognized the "vibration" of the presence. I even had a name for it. It was an angel, and I felt its name was Ariel. I actually felt I was being visited by an angel named Ariel, and it began to talk to me in my head. I couldn't tell if the angel was male or female or *both,* like a genderless spirit. "Do not be afraid of your physical body," it said. "Learn to have pleasure as you experience it. Your journey is to learn that. Tune in to the experience and drop your orientation of accomplishing a goal. The goal is the path."

Then the vibration seemed to dissipate, as though the angel had left. I replaced my backpack and continued to walk. The blister had formed on my right foot, which I knew was controlled by the left side of the brain. The left brain controls linear, logical thinking. It also is the mastermind of goal orientation. I knew that was my problem. Had Ariel been me speaking to myself, or had this angel been a separate entity—so to speak? Then I realized there was no difference. We were each everyone and everything, and everyone and everything was us . . . perhaps a mystical and esoteric point of view, but as far as I was concerned, the voice needed no more investigation. I would listen to it as long as it gave me good and reasonable advice—and if I didn't agree with what it was saying, I probably wouldn't hear it anyway.

So I continued to walk over the Pyrenees, oblivious of my blister, imagining how it had been, as I followed the old Roman road where the Arabs, the Romans, Charlemagne and his army, Napoleon, Saint Francis of Assisi, and millions of other pilgrims had trekked. I so longed to go back to those times as I struggled with the arduous, yet sublime, task of pushing ahead with pleasure.

Anna and I pressed past the French-Spanish border. The Spanish side was through a thick forest of beech trees, which ran alongside the north face of Mount Txangoa. At the collado de lzandorre, shortly after the ruins of Elizarra, I realized I would never be able to remember the names of all the places I encountered. I stopped at a drinking fountain—fountains, I would learn, would be waiting for me in every village. The pure, clean water of the village fountains in northern Spain made the Santiago Camino possible.

Walking over the Ibañeta Pass through more beech forests, we made our way into Roncesvalles. It was now nighttime. I had walked about twenty kilometers or nearly twelve and a half miles.

At Roncesvalles two great traditions meet: that of the pilgrim and that of the history and legend of Charlemagne. It was considered one of the earliest of the pilgrims' welcoming places and was funded down through the centuries by endowments from people of importance and wealth throughout Europe.

Roncesvalles had a mythical status among historians. It was a scene of many famous clashes between Charlemagne's and Aragonese and Basque armies. Here, in a great battle in 778, the Basque and Aragonese armies had massacred the rear guard of Charlemagne's army as it retreated. Here, too, Roland, the greatest of Charlemagne's paladins (the Twelve Peers) had died heroically. All this I knew from the reading I had done in preparation for the trek. But there was far more to learn, as I would soon discover.

* * *

Finally, Anna and I entered the *refugio* in Roncesvalles, exhausted and literally laughing with pain.

The barracks full of pilgrims was dark. Everyone was asleep, snoring and coughing. So this was how it was going to be? We each found a top bunk that was unoccupied and dumped our backpacks. Starving, we searched out the source of a light in a small backroom bar adjacent to the barracks. We entered the smoke-filled room where we were served oily mushroom soup. It made me gag, but we had no other food. Yes, this was how it was going to be.

We returned to the barracks and, because of the dark, couldn't find the shower. Filthy and caked with dirt and cold sweat, I climbed to my top bunk and fell into it. I stuffed earplugs into my ears and soon, to my surprise, fell asleep.

That night I think I dreamed about every man I had ever known. It was almost as though I was dreaming a cleansing of what had gone into these relationships. I was finished with them and ready to move on to some other way of operating with my sexuality. The dreams weren't really clear. They were montages of the baggage both I and they had brought to the various unions. I could sense that in each case neither of us had been whole. We were each looking for the other to fill a void in ourselves, rather than celebrating the fulfillment we had in ourselves—an attempt to find the lost other half of who we really were.

I was surprised at what I had dreamed. It seemed to have no relevance to what I had done that day.

I awoke to a German couple arguing loudly with each other. The rest of the barracks occupants tossed in disturbance.

How could a couple be so insensitive? I watched them for a while with my earplugs still in, like watching a scene underwater. Slowly the others got up, stretched, dressed, and left while the German couple continued to argue. They were heavyset and dense, oblivious of the difficulty they had created.

Anna and I took cold showers (there was no hot water), shaking our heads over the behavior of some people. I had read somewhere that "a pilgrim's way of being should be considerate, modest, self-sacrificing, friendly, grateful, never fussy or demanding, and at all times refraining from causing disturbance."

We decided that the German couple should be regarded as teachers and an invitation to eliminate judgment. Sure, I thought. I had a lot of learning to do.

*   *   *

After buying some yogurt and nuts from a small shop, Anna and I made our way to the Real Colegiata monastery, a thirteenth-century masterpiece of architecture, where we attended a mass for blessing the pilgrims. Although the mass was said in Spanish and I couldn't understand it, I found it very moving. We were told that Charlemagne's energy resided here because he had built a tomb on this site to commemorate his soldiers killed at the battle of Roncesvalles. I prayed and vowed to go all the way to the end of the Camino and let nothing stop me; an old modality, I thought to myself. Even at the beginning I was oriented toward the goal at the end. I thought of the bench in the Calabasas Mountains, but it didn't help.

As I marveled at the history around me, I felt someone's gaze on my back. I turned around and looked into the face of a startlingly handsome young man. He appeared to be in his mid-thirties, with a shock of dark hair, eyes like black olives, and bone structure that would look good on a stamp. He didn't avert his gaze.

I turned back around.

Anna and I finished our prayers and walked to a restaurant on a hillside. As we ate, the man from the church approached us. His body seemed to be vibrating as he sat down next to me. He spoke shyly in halting English and said, "I see something familiar in your eyes." Oh, brother, I thought, I'll bet. He then went on to say he was a volunteer helping pilgrims and asked if he could be of any service. I said no, I didn't need any service. He blinked and, getting my drift, left.

Anna winked, and we said no more.

We had our *carnés* stamped and looked around the town of Roncesvalles languidly, and then went to dinner. The young man showed up. He apologized for seeming to be forward and asked if I had a Knight Templar to ensure my safety on the Camino. I said no and I didn't think it would be necessary. He seemed to be speaking from another time and place. Then he broke the mold and went on to explain that he was glad he was the only one to recognize me and I had been his favorite actress since he was small. I chuckled because I was hearing that more than I wanted to these days. He said he was tongue-tied but because of his attraction to me, he couldn't help himself.

I was beginning to weaken. What was that dream the night before? A cleansing of the past?!

Anna discreetly left, and we talked some more. His name was Javier. He asked about my current romantic status. I said none. And then I found myself admitting that I had trouble being attracted to men my own age because they couldn't keep up. His eyes sparkled. His English improved, and we finished a lovely dinner. Then he became very concerned and almost paranoid about what others in the restaurant might think. It was strange.

I said I should be getting to bed and asked him if he would like me to write to him when I finished the Camino. He said no, it would upset his family. He said he wanted to walk with me on the Camino, but he had made a commitment to some people a few days up ahead. I said fine, and we got up and left the restaurant.

Then he said something really strange. Perhaps it was his English. "Shall we find a place to relieve ourselves?" he asked. I didn't know what he meant. Was he being archaic or vulgar? We had reached the front of a small hostel. A man came out. "You would like a room?" he asked. I wondered if it was all a setup. "No, thank you," I answered. "I need rest."

The young man looked at me, disappointment in his eyes. A gentle rain began to fall, accompanied by a breeze that almost spoke. Then he turned and walked away into an enveloping mist. "You are my fairy angel," he said as he disappeared into the fog. It was so lonely and dreamlike, I felt as though I had encountered another dream.

I thought of the Latino man on the trail in Calabasas. Were they both dreams I had manifested as real in order to understand something I had yet to learn?

I walked back to the communal confines of the *refugio*. Anna was ready for bed. She looked at me and simply said, "No?"

"No," I answered, and climbed to my top bunk, wondering what the hell was going on.

I tossed and turned in my sleep, questioning the role of sexuality in my life. A woman my age contemplating a quick and pleasant roll in the hay seemed unseemly. But why? Anna had said the Camino would offer me many experiences that I would choose or not choose to take. Was I so conservative and concerned with appearances in my advancing age that I blocked myself from spontaneity? I never used to be that way. What did age mean, anyway? I still had a good-looking body and was as interested in sex as the next person. Or was I?

Something had changed in me since my spirituality had become a physical part of my life. I could feel "energy" now, and it was more than activated hormones. I longed to "meld" with another person, not just have sex with him. But then the longing had actually dissipated.

I felt more complete in myself, and as I rifled through my sexual history, I was aware not only of how hormonally driven it had been, but also that each attraction had been based on some soul recognition. The hormones had served as a catalyst to investigate what each partner and I had had in common. With each person I had been aware of feeling something comfortably familiar, which usually led to a wondering discussion of whether that had indeed been true. Mythology talked about souls coming together again for various reasons, but some years ago I had determined for myself that it wasn't myth. I could honestly say that when I had recognized something deep in the soul eyes of a person, that was enough. It didn't matter what their interests were, how they looked, or whether they had anything in common with me today. If I recognized something from "yesterday," it was a motivating factor. It could be in the way he blinked his eyes, an expression of surprise when caught off guard, or anything that wasn't accompanied by self-consciousness or self-censorship for the sake of presentation. I was interested in what was underneath awareness. That was my sphere of attraction, and besides, it gave me something to investigate that kept me continually interested. I might have felt more comfortable with a "what you see is what you get" kind of person, but it wouldn't last long because there would be no mystery to explore, no connection of the spirit.

On reflection, I would say that I was usually attracted to "difficult to know" men. Men who wove elaborate schemes of obfuscation about who they really were. Together we would peruse each other until usually the man felt his privacy was invaded, and I was relentless in saying "So what." I was as anxious to have my own privacy understood as I was to understand my lovers' inner being. But men usually drew the line when they felt there was close to nothing left to hide. To me, that was what was wrong with the human race. Too many men hid their private agendas. In turn, frustrations built up until there was an explosion and they determined to become warriors of self-protection. At that point I would become bored (not liking to fight) and turn off. The men I had known would usually claim to have learned a lot about themselves ("stretched" was usually the word) and be relieved that I had gone away. But to me *they* had gone away. Away somewhere locked in the prison of themselves, only to find a woman who accommodated their fears and didn't challenge them to much growth. Being comfortable in a self-imposed prison was easier than really looking. Hence the female complaint that "men just won't express their feelings." I wondered if it wasn't a lot more complicated than that.

And now in my sixties, I was no longer interested in the game that accompanied so many relationships. If I was interested in a partnership at all, it would be with someone who felt the same way. What was there to protect except the truth? The truth not only of what had occurred in childhood and up to the present day, but of what had perhaps occurred even before this lifetime.

I had never pressed such inquiries in my past relationships, but I was ready to do that now. How else could we know who we really were? And wasn't that the reason to have intimate relationships anyway?

When I finally fell asleep, I dreamed I was on a horse riding into the sunset. I looked at myself in the dream. I seemed to be a person from another time, yet the path looked familiar. I was dressed in what appeared to be a gypsy dress with spangles and bright colors. I had long curly black hair and skin the color of a cappuccino coffee. I galloped on my horse, feeling free, yet I was running from something. Suddenly, I pulled up short and looked into the trees. There I saw Javier, the dark young man from that day. He didn't look the same, but I knew somehow that it was he. He was with a very white young maiden who did not want to be with him. He was frustrated at her attitude. He looked up at me on my horse, rose to his feet, and said, "I cannot do this. I never can. What is wrong?" He didn't speak in English, yet I could understand him. His eyes burned into my mind in the dream. He was trembling and longing for help. I looked behind me at whoever was chasing me. I leaned down and scooped him up onto my horse, wanting to rescue him from the place. I knew I knew him, but I didn't know why. He began to cry. I looked down at the white maiden. She was relieved and would be rescued by those who were pursuing me. With the young man riding behind me, I dug my heels into the horse's sides and galloped away. The last image in my dream was an objective view of myself, hair flying in the wind, galloping west, with the young man holding on around my waist. Following far behind, I saw soldiers covered in armor. The lead soldier carried a cross, which he held upright as he galloped west after me.

5

The next morning Anna and I set out for Zubiri. In pouring rain we trudged through mud, covered in waterproofed ponchos, looking like hunched-over witches with humpbacks. My poncho was yellow. Anna's was red. A collie dog, his long hair dripping with sparkling rainbow drops, stopped and stared as though he had never seen apparitions of this sort.

I loved the feeling of a portable waterproof house over me. I was a pilgrim, going slow, but getting there, a traveling turtle. We walked through fields of silent cows, herds of sheep, pigs, and horses. All stood as though in a water-soaked trance, not moving, not acknowledging us, somehow in a paradise of safety, knowing that all natural predators were in their own God-given moisturizing trance during the rain. It was nature's way of calling a truce for all potential disturbances. The animals seemed to understand an invisible harmony and had respect for each other's differences.

I could feel the walking stretching my spine while the backpack gently massaged my kidneys. I wasn't even aware of my blister. Maybe it had even gone away. I noticed a stick along the path and picked it up. It reminded me of the cane my mother had used in her old age. I stopped to tie my shoelace and walked off without the stick. Maybe it wasn't supposed to accompany me. No other stick spoke to me. Then a few miles later, I saw another one. It was crooked and, like a crescent moon, turned inward. I picked it up. It was good to lean on, even though it resembled a crone's discarded stock. I asked it if it wanted to walk with me . . . yes. I peeled away some of the hanging bark and made friends with it. I wanted to walk with this stick and didn't want to lose it. I decided to take it home with me if we made it to the end together.

The pain in my legs eased when I leaned on my new friend. I had a new guidebook too, which weighed two pounds, and I could feel it in my backpack.

Was suffering necessary for enlightenment? No, I thought, that's the old way of looking at life. Religious insistence on suffering was not supposed to be part of the New Age . . . not Christian, Moslem, or Hindu suffering. I thought of the jokes I had heard about the Hindu ascetic who finally reached the gates of heaven. He was given an ancient text to ponder before being let in. He understood the text until he came to a paragraph that made him cry. God asked him why he was crying. The old man looked at him and said, "But this says 'celebrate,' not 'celibate.'"

No, I would continue with my celebration of what was possible, understanding that my belief would create my reality, regardless of what had transpired down through the march of time in human history. Yes, I was simplistic and full of innocent wonder. I did not want to cave in to cynicism, and I didn't want to lose my sense of childlike optimism. I did, however, need to know what made me like I was. What was it that made me certain that what lay in my soul's knowledge was more real than my mind's knowledge?

I looked around as I walked. The hillsides were mystical, possessing treasures of experience that were there for us to hear if we would open up to them.

I began to slip in the mud as I leaned forward on my new friend, yet it kept me balanced, though it produced a cramp in my right shoulder. I reversed my stick to my left hand. I was not in as much control, but it would be good to learn to depend on my left hand as much as my right because it was, after all, connected to the feminine right side of the brain. The balance was necessary to be centered.

The forest was dotted with shimmering yellow marigolds. The sight of them reminded me that I hadn't seen a yellow arrow for hours. I had been too lost in my thoughts. Had I gone the wrong way? I looked around for Anna. She wasn't there. The rain obscured the view behind. Oh, God, I'm lost, I thought. And I was. I found myself on the edge of a muddy precipice. I remembered hearing that many pilgrims were injured on the Camino and often were forced to remain in *refugios* for weeks until they healed. Very few died, but it had happened.

I stopped. A sea of mud surrounded me. Okay. This was the polarity, I thought. One moment I was walking in paradise, the next in a small panic because I was lost, without my girlfriend, and in real danger of falling. I took a step. The mud was as slick as ice. Then I realized something was protecting me. I wasn't quite sure what it was. My stick seemed to retract when I attempted to plunge it into the thick mud. The earth itself seemed to have an intelligence that warned me against slippage. Was Mother Earth reaching out to help me? I remembered a walk in the California mountains. I hadn't realized that the sun would set so fast and found myself descending in the dark. Only it wasn't dark. The earth itself emitted a glow, just enough to light my way. I had been astonished, and when I told an Indian friend of mine, she said, "Oh, didn't you know that?" I felt stupid and unaware of nature's miracles. Now Mother Earth was nurturing me again. Why were we destroying her, disrespecting how much a part of each other we really were?

Very subtly, I felt my angel presence again. Ariel was with me, I thought. "Feel what it is to be alone," it said in my head, "to be stripped of so-called safety, to be one with nature, to be only with yourself." Then it was gone.

I took a deep breath and began to retrace my steps, certain now that I had bypassed the yellow arrow.

I must be diligent as I walk, I thought, looking backward every few yards to find the arrow. I must find a middle way of feeling, balanced and aware, yet allowing other dimensions to guide me.

I made my way back through the rain and mud. Through the birch trees, through the dense forest, up and down the slick hillsides, depending totally on my stick and the messages it received from the earth. The wind came up, pelting me with rain. I thought of the comfort of the *refugio*. The men snoring, the windows banging open and shut. I heard cars on a road not far away and remembered that I had heard that engine sound before.

I descended a mountain of loose rocks still upright. More boulders followed me into the riverbed below, mercifully missing me. Charlemagne and Saint Francis of Assisi went through this with hordes of armies and throngs of followers? What were they thinking? What made them do it? What was making me do it? Why was I here? Now, I was walking backward, retracing my steps. Was that the point? To retrace where I've been with another viewpoint? I looked up ahead. Anna was standing there, dripping in her red poncho. She waved. "Over here," she called. "Here is the yellow arrow." I trudged toward her, mud up to my calves.

"A trickster put the arrow going the wrong way," she said. "The Camino forces you to ascertain what is the truth and what is a human trick. Such is life, eh?" She chuckled. "I walked straight into a person's barn," she said. "A dog attacked me. I became incensed and screamed at him. He went away."

What would I do if a dog attacked me? I wondered. I had always had dogs in my life and thought I understood them. But what if I didn't?

Anna said if a dog attack ever got serious, she would stop and pray. I wondered if I would have the presence of mind and self-possession to do that. I had heard about the dogs on the Camino from reading books about it, one book in particular by a man who had apparently been attacked by a pack of dogs led by a particularly vicious black one. He wrote as though his life had been at stake. It happened in the abandoned village of Foncebadón, which lay ahead about two weeks' walk from where I now was. The dogs of Foncebadón had been the one true fear I had had in contemplating the Camino. I was genuinely terrified. . . . I would think about it later.

After resting for half an hour, Anna and I proceeded. What would I do without her companionship, someone who had done this thing, had been here before, someone who spoke Spanish and was reasonably confident? We followed the correct yellow arrow and climbed through pines, beeches, and oak trees. Before crossing the main road again, I saw a path of stones known as Roland's Footsteps, for the legendary knight who had sojourned here. The path of stones led to the former Venta del Puerto (Inn of the Pass), which was now a cowshed. Time was no respecter of history. It was up to humans to ferret out the past.

We passed a bridge leading to Zubiri and then a fountain adjacent to an ancient church. We stopped and filled our water bottles with the clear fountain water. So clear, so delicious. I sat by the fountain and put my feet up, concluding that all I really needed in life were good shoes, a loyal stick, and pure water.

✳   ✳   ✳

We arrived at a village some hours later and entered a bar filled with men and smoke. The men were screaming and yelling at a bicycle match on a small TV set. When we walked in, they turned around and applauded.

We had five miles to go before we reached the *refugio* in Zubiri. Could we make it before dark? I remembered the light of the earth in the California mountains, and as we trudged, I stopped to watch a humongous pile of dung where beetles had gathered to eat. They were all in the same place even though there were other piles of dung. Why didn't they spread out? They were something like the humans in that bar back there, or people who clustered around the pool in Florida when there was a spacious beach out there.

Up and down two more mountains we trekked. The rain had stopped.

When we reached Zubiri, there was no *refugio*. Somehow since Anna had been there, it had been disbanded and the old school, now used for pilgrims, was full. No room at the inn, so to speak.

It was now dark. In order to reach the next village, we needed to trek along the road for five more miles. The headlights of cars lit our way as we felt the windswept force of their passing us. They often honked their horns and cheered us on, yelling, *"Ultreya,"* from their windows.

"What does that mean?" I asked Anna.

"It means moving forward with courage," she answered.

6

We finally arrived in Larrasoaña at ten P.M. We had been walking since early morning in the mud and rain and had covered twenty-five kilometers—more than fifteen miles.

Everyone in the barracks was asleep, sounds of snoring and labored breathing echoing through the darkness. I found the cold-water shower, undressed, looked down, and saw that I had an open abrasion on the inside of my upper left thigh. Anna had some A and D ointment, which I applied. I thought I had brought everything I needed. There was no showerhead, just a hole where the water came out. I washed my hair, dried it as best I could with my little towel, which was already wet from having dried my body. I heard myself groan, and then I began to laugh. That made Anna laugh. Everything was so painfully preposterous.

Starving, we went into the "eating room" in the back of the *refugio*. Men were smoking and laughing. Someone gave us thick, oily soup with pieces of chicken floating in it. We laughed harder. This was why we were constipated. I had eaten nothing but prunes all day, but it hadn't helped. We laughed some more. We found our way back to the barracks, unfolded our sleeping bags, put them down on two lower cots. I put in my earplugs and fell down into sleep.

※　　※　　※

At six the next morning, I washed one pair of my socks and one pair of underpants in the cold-water shower and hung them on my backpack to dry as I walked. I used the toilet brush to clean my boots. I had already gotten into a time modality where I didn't want to waste a minute when I could be walking and accomplishing my goal to finish.

On the stretch to Pamplona, I began to walk faster than Anna. It was my natural rhythm. There were many other pilgrims who walked faster than I.

We passed villages with medieval churches that were and had been the center of people's lives for centuries. They were ornate and imposing and resonated with secrets of the past that I could feel from the walls.

On this land, it is said, Charlemagne and twenty thousand Christians had battled fifty thousand Moorish Saracens. The Saracens had hidden themselves for days before they ambushed Charlemagne's Christians. Twenty thousand people died in a few hours of battle over whose God was the true God.

Charlemagne's desire was to unify all of Europe under Christianity, and the Moors would die by the sword for Allah.

Nothing under the sun had changed much. The Camino had been the scene of Charlemagne's military pilgrimage. I wondered what Jesus would have thought of the noble Christian emperor and leader. The Camino that the early Christian saints had traversed had become a killing path. Yet it was called "the way" because whoever traveled it found his or her relationship to body, patience, food, water and feet and his or her orientation to distance and to God. Perhaps the act of *ultreya* should be reversed. Perhaps we should move *backward* with courage, so as to understand what we really came from and who we were.

I had had dreams and, of course, feelings of remembrances from the past of different times and places. I couldn't be sure of what they meant. I only know I have always felt a pureness of nostalgia about life experience being more than we think it is now. I don't like using the term *reincarnation* because it is so loaded with religious and perceptual prejudice. I'm not even sure that a past experience happened in the "past." I was beginning to become more and more aware of what Einstein had always claimed, that there is no such thing as linear time; we invented it. To me, I could feel things that might have occurred in the "past" but that were alive now, as though there was a time parallel in which different events occurred all at once. Why shouldn't all time be occurring at the same time? Why couldn't each of us be vessels of the totality of experience, which we simply choose to focus upon whenever we want?

At the age of seven, I remember standing on a piece of ground at Jamestown, Virginia, feeling absolutely certain that I had stood there hundreds of years before. The wind brushed across my face as though it had revisited me with that memory. Only it wasn't really a memory. It was happening to me at seven years old as a revisitation.

Such "memories" or revisitations had occurred for me in many parts of the world. I've always wondered if my love for travel hasn't been a desire to go home again to another place and time. In India I had known where temples and backstreets had been. In Russia I felt tearful when I looked at the Russian alphabet, which I knew I had once comprehended but couldn't read now. In Japan I knew I had been a geisha. And on and on. Was I retracing experiences I had already had in my own travels through time? Or was it possible to flick a time switch and click into any of those times and places *now?*

I remembered having an image of this that was simple and explicable to me. If I stood in front of a mirror and gazed at my entire body and that body was the containment of all of my experience, then I possessed the totality of my experience at that moment. If I focused on, let's say, one of my fingers, and only one of my fingers, then that finger would become the totality of my focus for the time that I focused. That finger, in effect, would become one experience, but that would not negate the fact that the rest of my experiences existed simultaneously in the totality of my body. That would mean that all my experiences were occurring simultaneously, although I was focusing only on one.

For me, this was not a problem of perception. I was not locked into linear reality. My reality encompassed everything simultaneously. Therefore, depending on my mood or desire for adventure, I could dip into simultaneous realities whenever I tuned into them. Sometimes I felt I had no control over reactivating the focus. Dreams seemed beyond my control, yet when I analyzed the dream state, I realized that on some level I must be controlling in some manner what I dreamed. In other words, my subconscious was manipulated by the superconsciousness in order to give myself more clues as to who I was. My higher consciousness was connected to God (the source, creation), and existed to remind me (my conscious and subconscious) that I also was a totality of experience that was connected to God.

Then I found myself on the Camino in Spain, where so much killing had occurred in the name of humankind's connection to God.

Why here?

I had always loved period pictures. There was something familiar to me in them that I loved to look at: the dress, the morals, the way of life. Anything to do with the past was an entertainment both emotional and familiar to me, although I never thought I could successfully enact a character from the deep past because I seemed too modern to myself. It was as though I knew I couldn't go there again, even in acting, because I remembered how it had actually been and didn't want to denigrate it with a fantasy Hollywood overlay.

I had the same fascination with the future and the presence of other worlds inhabited by beings that I also had a familiarity with. So to me, the past and the future were part of me now. There was nothing wacky or preposterous about knowing the lines of time such as I understood them to be. They just *were,* like nature or the sky. In other words, I felt that time existed in me rather than that I existed in time.

As I walked the Camino, I asked myself why I had come to do this. Was I, in effect, walking backward in a time that already existed in me? Yes, I thought. I have been here.

The image of myself as the coffee-skinned, black-haired girl in my dream came up again. With each step she became clearer. She rode horseback over this road. She was free, but always running from something chasing her. She didn't want to be noticed until it was *her* decision. I had so many of these feelings today. I had loved being a public movie star when the professional requirements of publicity were there. But I had developed many escape routes in my private life to fool the press, the paparazzi, or anyone who would invade my private life. I seemed to be wearing my life like an open book with my candidness and writings, but there was so much that I had been wily about concealing.

Even in my travels, I had somehow been proficient at avoiding dangerous situations—escaping a coup d'état in Bhutan, eluding the Communist authorities in the Soviet Union, living with the Masai in East Africa, protecting myself in the Peruvian Andes, and so on. My life had indeed been an evolutionary learning exercise.

Those thoughts meshed together in my mind as I walked. Had I learned the techniques of escape and survival from the black-haired girl?

As I walked, I somehow felt the energy of the path talking to me. The black-haired girl swam more clearly into my understanding. She was Moorish, and she had the gift of healing with her hands. She traversed the Camino on horseback, tending the sick. Then I saw her with a giant sultan of some type. The Giant Moor, they called him. She was called into his presence. I could feel the scene. I melded into it, until I was as one with it; I *was* the Moorish girl, and I was in a Moorish palace. I couldn't make out the details. I related more to the feelings. The Moor had summoned me to heal him from a problem with impotence. He had many courtesans and couldn't satisfy them. I was ordered to heal his problem. And I remembered how I had looked into his eyes. It felt as though my eyes were his, which were jet black but sparkling with emotion. I felt myself go into those eyes, remaining still for a long time. He relaxed. Then I lifted my hands to his shoulders. He didn't blink. I used the gift of skin touch with my hands all over his body. His protectors looked on. I dipped my hands in oil stored in a keg made of animal skins. Our eyes never averted from each other. He was pliable and wanted to understand. He succumbed to the vibration of my touch and soon became aroused. His protectors left as I proceeded to consummate the healing. The Giant Moor sighed and was grateful and rested comfortably. I lay beside him.

In a few hours he sat up. He said he wanted me to remain with him. I refused, pleading that my destiny was on the Camino in a healing capacity. He became infuriated, called for his protectors, and had me thrown into prison, where I found myself among Christian women. They were pale and starving and wailing and full of hatred for their Moslem captors. All this I saw while I was walking. I was in a kind of dream-walking meditation. The recall ended abruptly. I was stunned.

Then I thought of the world today. I thought of Bosnia and Yugoslavia, and Christian versus Moslem hatred. I thought of Iraq and Saddam Hussein and the mullahs in Iran and the chasm that had been born out of ancient hatred between Moslems and Christians. I thought of the simmering Middle Eastern hatred between Arab and Jew and the birth of monotheism during the forty-year wanderings of the Jews with Moses in the desert. And, I wondered, once monotheism had come into being as a theological reality, had Mohammed heard the same Voice that Moses had heard? Why did everyone think that his God was the only God? And more interesting than all of that to me was the role that sexual prowess, competence, and aggression had played in the annals of human history. Somehow, sexual identity was tied to God. Why?

A logging truck nearly clipped my backpack as I walked along a busy highway, living two realities simultaneously. The Camino was ancient and modern at the same time. The modern engineers seemed to know that the energy of the Camino provided the best place to construct a road. Saints and soldiers spanned the two extremes of those who experienced the "way." Was the "middle way" possible in this world? Each of us seemed to have extreme views, in one way or another, and always the extremes were clashing. Was that how we "learned" about being respectful of *all* views?

I still hadn't eaten anything but prunes and Emergency C, which I dumped in my water bottle. Anna was existing on Coca-Cola and cigarettes. Both of us pushed on. I never told her what was swimming in my head.

When we reached Pamplona, we found a *refugio* in the basement of a church.

That night I had nightmares. I was falling from mountains, drowning in streams and rivers, sliding and pitching over rocks.

I was hurt and alone, fearful that no one would find me and help. Was I dreaming the present or the past?

When I woke up, I found Anna sitting on her bunk bed packing. I knew she was going to leave me.

"Point your finger at me," she said. "Pretend you are accusing me of something."

I pointed at her. "You see, you have three fingers pointed simultaneously at yourself?"

"Yes," I answered.

"So when we judge another, we are really judging ourselves. There is no difference."

"You are leaving today, aren't you?" I asked.

"Yes," she answered. "You need to be on your own from now on. That is the point of the Camino."

I was on the edge of crying. I remembered how I felt when I left home at sixteen years of age. I thought of how my daughter must have felt when she was put on a train for boarding school. Her attempt to keep control of her emotions so bravely had reduced me to tears as I waved good-bye to her.

Now I was being put out on my own as well, in a strange country with a strange language. But maybe it wasn't so strange. Perhaps I was here to find that truth. I had a sense that I would be false in the world, wearing a mask that blinded and disoriented me, unless I knew more deeply what had gone before.

"The Camino will show you the past and the future until you realize who you are now," said Anna. "You will have no other diversions as you walk alone ten hours every day. Be aware and diligent as you walk and contemplate. I will check in on you."

I couldn't speak. I didn't want to show the fear I had of my own inadequacies. What would I do if there was no one to help me? And what would I do if people recognized me and became *too* helpful?

Anna fastened her backpack around her waist, hugged me, walked out of the church basement, and was gone.

7

I choked back tears and quickly gathered my things, put on my backpack, and walked up some stairs and onto the streets of Pamplona.

I walked alone for a while, not sure whether I was going in the right direction. West, I thought. I should just walk west. People scurried through the city, busy with their jobs and lives. I was not one of them; I was outside of them; I was a pilgrim who had no knowledge of anything to do with the world around me. I felt isolated and paralyzed. It was worse than if I had been in the loneliness of the countryside, because here in the city I felt self-conscious.

I was used to having an identity and a role to fulfill in a city. In the peace of the countryside, I could meld into nature, even if I had nowhere to go.

I walked for a while, not even aware I was moving. What was my purpose right now, at this moment? Was it to find a yellow arrow? Then I spotted three women a few blocks ahead of me. They were wearing backpacks from which hung scallop shells. I knew they were pilgrims too. I got hold of myself and tried to catch up to them. They were speaking rapid-fire Spanish. I followed them for a while. They were crossing Pamplona looking for a yellow arrow too. Suddenly they stopped. They had found it. It led to a direction out of town. I knew I was on the right track for the time being. I felt better. The women walked on, and I headed for a phone booth. I looked at my reflection in a store window. I looked pitiful.

After much confusion as to how to make an international phone call on the street, I succeeded in calling Kathleen in London.

When she answered, I told her what I felt . . . a kind of sorrowful, humbling bravery. She said she was feeling the same way. "I'm taking Ken's ring off now," she said. "You do the Camino for me. I'm leaving this life soon, and you are finding a new one. I'll be walking with you." Her voice began to tremble, and she gently hung up.

I hung the phone on its cradle and listened to the sounds of the traffic. Then I watched myself in the store windows as

I trudged on to the next town, listening to the pealing of church bells.

I passed the cathedral in the heart of the ancient Navarrería district. A traditional site of pilgrims' worship along the Camino, and magnificent with its many chapels and the museum containing works of art from the cathedral and other churches of the region, including sculptures and manuscripts. Bloody battles had occurred on the ground where I walked, commemorated by many churches as reminders of Pamplona's violent medieval past. The Church of Santo Domingo was decorated with scallop shells and a statue of Saint James looked over the high altar.

I followed the yellow arrows across the outskirts of Pamplona, wondering out loud to my stick about the history of this blood-soaked terrain during the Middle Ages. I decided my stick was male and would know how to cross Spain by itself.

Back again in the countryside, I continually looked down so I wouldn't miss the yellow arrows. There were many discarded cigarettes along with plastic bags, papers, cartons, and condoms. How could people trash such sacred land? Would I discard my possessions later if my backpack became too heavy?

A dump truck passed me. I remembered my trip to the "city of garbage" in Egypt. People lived in a place where refuse was dumped. My Western friends had been horrified. I had seen a resigned peace in the eyes of the inhabitants, who had nothing. I walked for a time thinking of the burden of possessions and the need to be identified by what one owned. I felt a freedom in knowing that my survival and probable evolution depended on owning only what I needed. That was the question, though—how much did a person need? I remembered hearing a story, possibly apocryphal, about Mother Teresa's insistence that a plush hotel accommodation be stripped bare at a cost of one hundred thousand dollars so that she could stay there in poverty. There was something wrong with that.

I leaned against a tree on my stick, looking out at villages and hamlets in the distance, listening to crows cawing. Wheat fields nestled in misty valleys. I was beginning to trust the earth itself. I remembered that my father had told me that his mother had taught him how to fear, and once he had gone on a trip with his money belt strapped around his waist. I was doing the same thing, just in case I needed it.

I prayed to Ken that he would enlist God's help in curing Kathleen's illness. I could almost feel him refuse because he wanted her with him. I remembered Kathleen telling me that he had said that proof of her love for him would be for her to come down to the bottom with him. I guess that even included going up to heaven.

A huge caterpillar crossed my feet. I watched it on its own camino, wondering when it would become a butterfly.

My left hip was numb. There was no pain. Was it a pinched nerve?

I heard countryside church bells, and their sound made me think of my childhood in my father's hometown of Front Royal,

Virginia, nestled in the Shenandoah Valley. There were arguments in our family over whether the Methodists or the Baptists were the true link to God! Limited perspectives abounded everywhere.

When I arrived in the Puente La Reina *refugio,* I met two Irish girls who were cooking noodles and sausage on a cooker they carried with them. They recognized me, said my books had inspired them, and proceeded to sing Irish songs and play the flute as though to dispel the Spanish surroundings. They talked incessantly, which disturbed me. I could feel myself pointing a finger with three directed at myself.

They had lovely singing voices though, and I was reminded of the story Anna had told me about a young man along the Camino who had a beautiful singing voice but was too shy to speak, much less sing. At the end of his Camino, a big celebration had been planned at the church, but the priest had failed to come. The other pilgrims begged the boy to sing. He sang so beautifully they all wept. His fellow pilgrims knew he had accomplished a turning point because of his pilgrimage.

I began to notice that the Irish girls and others in the *refugio* were relating to me as a privileged actress from Hollywood. I wanted to be treated like everyone else, but found it difficult to embarrass them with that request. Anna had said, "Remember you are simply not like the others who walk the Camino. You carry your own baggage of celebrity. Prepare for that."

I spent some time thinking about that celebrity baggage that accompanied me whenever people recognized who I was.

True, they would confide their most personal feelings to me because somehow I engendered a trust that they felt they could depend upon. But I rarely felt they were being their true selves. They usually presented a version of themselves that they wished me to see, including what they thought of me. I longed to know more than their deepest secrets. I wanted to know the aspects they weren't orchestrating. I had been a "celebrity" since I was twenty years old and had for the most part been exposed to people who related more to me than they did to themselves and each other. Regular people don't like celebrities to see their faults. However, they are quite free about sharing their deepest fears and secrets. Maybe it's because they know we have been through being exposed in public and can trust that we are sensitive to their issues of pain.

I found myself shy to sing along with the Irish girls because I was a musical performer and I didn't want to be anything other than regular. All human beings sing at one time or another, but I somehow didn't feel free from performing.

After our singing meal, I discovered how to zip open my sleeping bag from the bottom and fell asleep in it.

When I awoke, I decided to discard a sweater and one pair of socks. My life had become the burden of what I was carrying.

The celebrity burden reared its head as I began the next day.

A photographer waited outside the *refugio,* camera in hand. The Irish girls immediately stepped protectively in front of me and told him to go away. The other pilgrims were bewildered.

The Irish girls assumed the role of my protectors and walked ahead of me for the next few days. There were journalists in the mountains. The Irish shooed them away. But I could tell the word was out. The girls seemed to enjoy their new role as bodyguards. It relieved the tedium of walking. I was walking in two worlds. One of peace and meditation and the other of anticipation that the serenity would be compromised.

I randomly opened my small copy of the New Testament as Anna had suggested. There it was: Acts 9, the story of Saul on the road to Damascus. He saw the light. Would I? What was I expecting to happen to me on this pilgrimage? No other pilgrim I spoke to could explain why he or she was walking. It was a subject that came up every night in the *refugios*. There had been an impulse, almost a compulsion, that had guided us to drop our lives, put everything in suspension, and come to Spain, and none of us knew why. Some had actually *escaped* to the Camino. One Danish man had walked in on his wife with another man, so he took his dog and came to Spain to figure out his life. Another woman was ill with arthritis and thought she might be cured by the exercise and the energy. But no one really understood his or her soul's reason. There was something deeper than NOW, and everyone discussed it.

I walked in wheat fields waist deep, then through apple groves with the wind whipping dappled sunlight on the leaves.

A couple from Holland seemed weighed down from possessions, as though they were refugees from a war.

I lost the Irish girls, missed a bridge, and got lost for a day. It didn't bother me at all. My sense of smell increased, and because I was lost, there was no press.

I had begun to feel blissful, moving gently forward in a meditative state of mind, when a dog jumped out of nowhere and made no secret that he wanted me out of the way. He blocked my path. I couldn't go backward, and I couldn't go sideways. The path was too narrow. I was suddenly faced with what had always frightened me. He barked at me unmercifully. I realized then that, unlike Anna, I wasn't the type to stop and pray at a moment like this. I thought quickly. I raised my trusty stick and remembered what my Hopi friend had told me: "Visualize a red heart, fill it with love, and project it toward the dog without feeling hostility." I formed a red heart in my mind, filling it with as much love as I could muster, and sent it out to the dog. I still had my stick raised, however, and I decided I would step off the path, even though there was underbrush and obstacles, and go around him. He growled, but I kept visualizing the heart and I kept walking. He looked at me curiously and watched me get back on the path. As soon as he saw I was on my way and had maneuvered around him, he lunged for me again, just for good measure. I ran from him with my backpack thumping up and down. He chased me for a while. I kept running until he gave up.

I stopped, and when I looked back, he was out of sight. Breathing deeply and sore with another blister, I began to compare the similarities of dogs and the press. They each traveled in packs, and they each "pressed" you to understand the truth as you saw it.

I had always been quite friendly with journalists, having lived with two very good ones for many years, admiring their curiosity and overriding need to learn about other people's truth. The Fourth Estate kept civilization honest. Yet they could become brutally invasive, and out of a need to sell papers or get TV ratings, they often jumped the gun. But the public's insatiable addiction to celebrity news contributed as much to tabloid insanity as anything else. The journalists I knew were usually fair and made a point of checking their sources. However, when it came to journalistic reportage on metaphysical or spiritual matters, they fell short of fairness, a prejudice based almost completely on their feeling threatened by the subject themselves. Most journalists are not interested in self-investigation; they labor under the illusion that their beliefs must not influence their objectivity. The sarcasm that they feel it necessary to display only says more about them than it does about the person they investigate. So my experience with the press had been mostly positive when they related to me as part of their "real" world—my acting, my political activism, my interest in traveling, or even my writing on stress reduction through meditation. But when it came to my interest in physical reembodiment or healing through past-life therapy, or my speculations on UFO activity and other matters that weren't scientifically acknowledged as "real," then negativity reigned. And when a movie critic reviewed a part I'd played in relation to what past life I might be portraying, it was yellow journalism that didn't become his profession.

Dogs are like journalists. They test your truth. If I was walking blissfully thinking I was at one with God, with my feet on the ground and my head in the stars, the snarling dog or journalist certainly tested how peacefully enlightened I really was. I saw that in a flash. I hoped I would improve. I can say that that particular dog engendered my deepest respect and motivated me to think long and hard about how my fear could be quelled, especially since I had the dogs of Foncebadón ahead of me.

The press would be more complicated to deal with. They felt comfortable denigrating the spirituality of human emotions. When science said nothing could be proved through intuition or spiritual belief, the press went along with that. If science said objective observation was not possible through consciousness—giving short shrift to psychic insight, saying it was an enlightened accident at most—the press agreed.

The press and science had no real respect for feelings in the world. They each preferred collective observations and called that consensus *fact*. It was as though scientists and journalists never gave themselves permission to be human. Indeed, *they* were the aliens in human society, seeking to establish by consensus a new race dependent on them who had no capacity to feel. If a person was not "rational" by their definition or scientifically inclined, he or she was ostracized.

Spirituality is the authentic discovery of one's capacity to feel. You could define it as a theopathic state, and when your emotions align with the Divine, you understand more of who you are. A revitalization of basic emotional truths occurs.

Religion attempted to satisfy those longings by molding a person's beliefs and behavior into a form that is acceptable to society. Religion attempted to chain the domain of human feeling, resulting in people who are no more than architectural shells. Science sought to shed itself of the emotional and spiritual, seeking a consensus of knowledge and facts. Science felt that emotions undermined objectivity. It seemed to me that objectivity never existed anyway. Reality is always a question of individual perception.

I was seeing that the Camino itself was a history of religious factions, each of whom claimed to have spiritual superiority. But so many human beings had been jailed by the Church in the name of Christianity, no matter how violent; and now science was the jailer of spirituality, no matter how dismissive.

The press reported from the point of view of the wardens of each prison, while claiming objectivity.

What is unique about human beings is our awareness of feeling. The press conspired to ridicule that and thereby smother it.

The true courage of individualism is the ability to follow one's passion. The real aliens are those who are alienated from the ability to champion feeling. If we could make peace with our individual emotions, we could not be manipulated to kill. If our institutions don't help us discuss our feelings, we may disrespect and ultimately turn away from them, probably with violence.

It is mankind's moral obligation to seek joy through the feeling of Divinity within his or her own being.

I think I was walking the Camino to feel human again.

In the town of Estella on the way to Los Arcos, I stopped in a shop to get a less recognizable hat and a tube of Erace to cover my sunburn. Vanity was ever present. I developed a muscle strain in my right leg. I also was beginning to smell the sweat accumulating in the capoline fabric of my shirt. Cotton was sweeter, but it didn't dry as fast as capoline. The breeze flicked away perspiration, but the smell was pungent. I am a fastidious person, particularly about smelling good. This was fundamentally unpleasant for me.

I got some new beeswax earplugs because they fit the interior of my ears more comfortably.

As I was leaving the town, my eye caught a newspaper. There I was on the front page! My hat and backpack were immediately identifiable. Quickly, I put on my new hat and kept walking. No one noticed.

I was now feeling the first pangs of a desire to flee. Fleeing anywhere so I could be alone and unrecognized. The Irish girls were ahead a few miles. I hurried to the countryside and found a tree to sit under. Soon I fell asleep against my backpack. . . .

Images coursed through my head. I was upset. Then something happened that I didn't really understand. I was not really dreaming, yet I don't know how else to define what transpired. I was running on the trail, dark, slim, with black hair, and dressed in the same wardrobe as in my dream before. Only this seemed more than a dream. It seemed both familiar and intensely real. I was trying to elude soldiers who were fighting each other. One group of soldiers was Caucasian and carried a cross as they fought. The others were dark-skinned and fought with long knives. They wore colorful robes and spoke in a language that I thought was mine, though I couldn't understand it. I ran through the forest until I saw a campfire. Another soldier of the cross heard me, stopped me, and took me into an encampment. I knew the camp was a "Christian" one. One of the soldiers leered at me and another came forward to approach me. He was drunk and laughing. I stood looking at him, not knowing how to react. Then a man in a monk's robe came out of the shadows. He stepped between me and the leering soldier and led me into a tent. A candle flickered inside.

"I am John the Scot," he said with an archaic Scotch-Irish lilt. "You have beautiful skin."

I felt prideful, somehow totally void of fear. I heard myself say to him, "You have skin the color of the tallow of candles."

He sat down and began to massage his huge feet. He was bulky and rotund with freckled white skin and deep, yet mischievous, blue eyes.

"You are not part of the Moorish resistance here on the trail?" he asked.

"No," I answered. Then I began to explain. "I am Moorish, but with a Hebrew heritage. The truth is unknown to me, yet I know the Koran and the Kabbala represent the same truth. I am an herb healer. I respect the cross, but what lies between a soldier's legs is not a gift to me. I speak the language of my mother's ancestors—Hebrew."

I was fascinated at hearing my own strange words. Where was this coming from?

The monk just gazed at me. I felt the need to explain further.

"It is ironic to me that armies seek to kill each other over whose truth is primary. And why do the Christians seek out the remains of Saint James, who was a Jew? This Camino is a journey of the body longing to join itself in spirit, not separated from itself as in the case of Saint James and his head."

The monk motioned for me to sit across a small table from him. The candle lit his ruddy, intelligent face.

"You can read and write?" he asked.

"Most certainly," I answered.

"What separates you from the other heathens and pagans?" he asked.

"The same thing that separates me from a fool!" I answered.

"And what is that?" he asked.

"This table, sir," I answered.

He laughed.

The ensuing dialogue was murky to me. I remember subjects and issues and my feelings regarding what was said more than the details of our conversation. We talked of the necessity for education. He agreed, and we talked with some knowledge of the movements of the stars in astrological terms. I knew that such a science was very well respected in those days. He said he was well versed in old Roman texts and because of that knew the location of the sepulcher of Saint James. He said that as a cleric he wished to work with me in obtaining many texts that were located in the libraries in Alexandria, which the Moors controlled. He knew that many texts had been preserved and wished for me to help him obtain them so that he would bring them to the court of Charlemagne, where he served as a mentor-educator to the illiterate king of the Franks. He said many of Charlemagne's courtiers were illiterate, which was why he had been brought from Scotland and Ireland. The ancient texts had been preserved there with secret works about God, which Charlemagne was interested in.

Then I dreamed that he reached into a corner and produced a staff of some kind.

"This is a Druidic staff," he said. "It is empowered with energies from meditation and prayers. It has also been dipped in the ancient wells that we believe contain the spirits of the saints."

He handed me the staff. I gently pounded it on the earth floor of the tent. I liked the feeling of it in my hand. It seemed friendly. John went on.

"I am Scots-Irish and was born and grew up in the place where the Book of Kells was written."

At that moment two more monks came in. They were men, but they had the faces of the two Irish girls I had met on the trail.

"These clerics will protect you," he said. "They will shield you from those who 'press' you."

Then something occurred that baffled me, as though in my own "dream-vision" I was dreaming along a time line. John the Scot spoke, and as he did, I was reliving the past as well as a future dream. There was no linear sequence, only events and pictures, which were narrated by him.

"You will be captured by the Giant Moor," he said. "He will initially use you for healing, but when you spurn his advances, you will be placed in a dungeon. He will summon you from time to time to discuss healing and to argue the meaning of God. You will give him your understanding of Christianity. You will then be liberated by the Christians upon his death."

I saw the pictures in my head as John described them, but I had already dreamed this imprisonment a week ago.

"The Moor will be defeated by Roland, the right-hand soldier-servant of Charlemagne. As the Moor dies, he will ask for me. He will give me a small golden cross and ask that I give it to you for protection. The cross will be constructed in such a way that it could be interpreted as Coptic, Christian, or Islamic-

Egyptian, which is a symbol of good luck. Much religious trick-
ery is used along the Camino, in order to please the God of the
enemy in case of capture. In any case, you will be freed."

I saw the scene he described. The knight Roland was
smaller by half than the Giant Moor. They fought one another
with sticks and clubs in hand-to-hand combat, almost good-
naturedly, under the sunshine, up against a wall. The Moor was
more than seven feet tall. His weight and size tired him. At one
point he picked up Roland and placed him on his horse. They
both laughed. The giant then put down his weapon and asked
for some time to rest. He and Roland then began a searching
dialogue about whether Christianity or Islam was the true religion. They debated for some hours. Neither would give in to
the other. They agreed that whoever defeated the other would
serve to represent the superior religion. They then discussed at
some length the Giant Moor's invincibility. Roland questioned
his opponent's invulnerability to the sticks, stones, swords, and
arrows with which they fought. The giant then confessed that
if he were ever run through with a sword in the navel, it would
be his undoing.

Then they both agreed to sleep. I saw Roland place a stone
under the giant's head for comfort. In respect for the conven-
tions of chivalry, they both agreed there would be no more
combat until after they rested.

Sometime later they both woke at the same moment. They
resumed combat. Roland grasped the giant under the chin to

throw him off balance. They both fell to the ground. They pulled themselves up and remounted their horses. They proceeded to run through each other's horses with swords. The animals were badly wounded. Each man dropped his sword. They fought again with stones and fists. Neither fell. Darkness came. They called another truce and slept through the night. The giant was tired the next morning. Each seemed to have deep respect for the other's bravery. Roland awakened before the giant. He sought out the giant's own sword, and then the giant woke. He didn't notice that his sword was missing. Instead, they again argued about whose God was the true God. The anger between them intensified, and when the giant looked in another direction, Roland ran his sword through the giant's navel. As the Giant Moor lay dying, he asked for John the Scot. John, who had witnessed the battle, appeared. The Moor took a cross from his robes and handed it to John with the request that he give it to me. He had used it for negotiating purposes whenever he or his men were in skirmishes with Christians.

As I was dreaming, I began to cry. When I looked closely into the face of the Moor, it became the face of my company manager, Mike Flowers. Then I found myself back in the tent listening to John.

"You see," said John, "Mr. Flowers is now your trusted associate who is repaying a debt for himself."

I cried again. I felt I needed to adjust to what John had said, but he went on with his discourse. He said that so many wars had been fought along "the way" because the energy beneath the ground amplified all human emotions. He said the Camino accentuated feelings of unresolved issues—feelings of hate, anxiety, fear, sexual desire, and love—because they were amplified. He said the energy intensified karma between opposing forces. He said there were ley lines placed there long ago for reasons that I would learn later. He said the ley lines were directly aligned with the constellations of stars, which would help resolve conflicts if properly understood. He said the dreams and visions of people walking the trail created footmarks of past truth, which created reminiscences, which were part of the human subconscious lurking within each of us as foreshadowings.

He said people always return to old haunts because they intuit that the karma there needs to be resolved.

Then he got specific in my dream-vision. "The young man whom you met at the beginning of the trail is quite mad. He had been wounded in a battle in which you tried to help him. You attempted to save his life with your herbs. Yours was the last face he saw as his soul slipped out of his body. He had loved you, yet that love was unconsummated. None of his loves had been consummated because he didn't know how to love. He was a warrior. He never knew how to be complete within himself because he never knew God within himself. If one does not feel love for animals and birds and fishes or cool breezes upon the skin, one never knows the God within. Without knowing that, one cannot really love another. Thus, the young man turns women away with his sexual passion. But his soul recognized you today."

As John the Scot spoke, I saw the face of Javier looking up at me as I tended him. Suddenly, his face was transformed until it became the face of the Hispanic man on the trail in Calabasas. John continued to explain. "Both individuals suffer from a lack of cohesion between physical love and soul love. You will understand the more ancient reasons for this later."

In my dream-vision I became confused about time. I was existing at the end of the twentieth century, yet having an experience in the eighth century, in the time of Charlemagne, while this John the Scot dream I was dreaming seemed itself to be going backward and forward in time.

The vision went on in linear fashion. I saw myself as the Moorish girl released from Moorish captivity and being tutored by John. I lived among the Christian soldiers along the Camino, who continually taunted me with sexual innuendo, yet I was protected by John.

Then I was bathing in a stream. I found it too cold and tiptoed out of the water, where I was confronted by several Christian soldiers at the water's edge. I stood my ground but was anxious. Out of the forest came John. He had been watching. He walked over to me and began chanting incantations that were associated with baptism rituals. With his huge arms, John pushed me back into the water and shoved my head under. I came up sputtering and shouting in Arabic. John understood my protestations because he spoke Arabic, but the soldiers didn't.

Then I heard him tell them that I was having a holy vision and he was baptizing me as a Christian and they should depart immediately. They left.

He pulled me from the stream and placed a gold cross on a chain around my neck. It was the gold cross the Moor had given him.

"You wore that cross for the rest of your life," John said. "Because while no one could truly be sure of whether you were Christian, Moslem, or Jewish, it saved your life. No one could afford to accost you or arrest you on either side of the lines of religion. You traveled up and down the trail, having many experiences, and that is why you are here today. Many need resolution."

John the Scot was sitting across the table from me, telling me about a future in *that* time period, yet it was all happening as I dreamed *now*.

He then narrated further into the future. "I took you to the court of Charlemagne, where you garnered respect and became an advisor to the court, after the Moorish influence and their borders were stabilized."

Almost as a flash-forward simultaneously with a flashback, I saw myself in the medieval court. I wore the Christian garb, but with my long black hair and dark skin, I willingly called attention to myself. I became friendly with the king and spent many hours with him on animal skins in front of a massive fireplace. John said the king had had three or four wives and many, many mistresses. He was lusty and adored women. He loved to swim, and I saw myself in a warm-water pool fed by a fresh spring. We frolicked with underclothing on and talked of Moorish poetry, which I translated for him because of his illiteracy. He was a proud man, but unself-conscious about his education. He wished to understand the Islamic God as opposed to the God of his pope. He spoke of the pope with deep love and respect and said he was devoting his life to his wishes. He said he had promised his father to toil for the church in Rome.

I wore my gold cross at all times. John told me it represented the balance of the earth in all four directions and whoever held it anchored himself to the earth plane, which would provide him with all the joys and sorrows of the earth's existence.

I saw myself with a retinue of attendants, traveling the Camino in a carriage protected by soldiers and horses.

"You often visited your homeland," said John. "You collected Moorish scrolls and texts and brought them back to Charlemagne's court, where you and I and the king would pore over their meaning."

I saw the group of us by firelight that flickered against stone walls, translating the writings of Arab sages, arguing over God and the meaning of warfare relating to God's love. Then I saw the king ask for permission from the court that I be formally recognized as one of his mistresses. They refused because of my heritage. He openly declared his love for me and wished

to demonstrate it. He took the entire court to the seaside at
high tide and claimed that his love was as powerful as the tide.
"One can never hold back either love or the tide," he said. The
court was impressed and allowed me to be a consort, but nothing more. I knew I was one of many. I had lovers as well, but
nothing meant as much to me as learning, not even the king.

I spent many hours with John the Scot debating the great
truths of each religion. He was liberal and funny, and I saw us
arguing a great deal, until the king's shadow would appear at
the great wooden door and he would insist he needed me in
his chambers. There were tables laden with fruits and nuts and
always the monstrous wall fire illuminated his face.

The king knew, and wanted to know more, about the
movement of the stars. He acted as though he were a teacher,
but, in truth, was a pupil, curious about all things.

He wore a fabric shirt next to his skin, and the same fabric made up his leggings. Wrappings held tight by bands covered his leggings. Soft leather boots encased his feet. When he
was cold, he wore a kind of leather tunic next to his chest.
When I watched him dress for a public appearance, he donned
a blue cloak which he slung over his shoulder. A sword with a
gold hilt hung from his waist, and he wore a crown of gold and
jewels. He also had a jeweled sword that he wore at feasts and
celebrations, concealed by robes of embroidered fabrics.

"You bore him three children," said John. "You lived to be
eighty-three years of age and were upset to see your children

disinherited after their father's death because of their Arabic blood." I listened, and as I gazed at John, I felt as though I was in a dream within a dream. Then, as though he were speaking to me in the present day, he said, "You reacquainted yourself with the soul that was then Charlemagne, in the life you live now."

I tried to comprehend what that meant. I said, "You mean I met him again in this lifetime I'm living now?"

"Most certainly," he answered.

"Well, who is it?" I asked.

John's eyes became kind and yet mischievous. "My child, you will know that when you accomplish a bit more of your struggling Camino. That is what it's for, now, isn't it?"

"I'm not sure what anything is for at this point in time," I said, "because I don't even know what time is."

"Precisely," said John.

I didn't know how to go on, either on the trail or in the dream-vision.

John spoke again. "Remember the trail enables you to recall who you are. You are the repository of many experiences along the road of time. And as you move forward, you are in effect going within, which you would term going backward in time. In truth, you are seeking to travel forward to the beginning. *Ultreya* ... have courage, because all roads lead to the beginning. You will see some of that in due course. Thus you must travel your road, out of time, until you make the symmetrical loop of understanding what went before. All lines loop back to the beginning."

I felt a wind against my face, and with a shiver, I came to. I looked around. I was still sitting against the tree and alone. I was safe. There was no press. I looked at my watch. I had been in this state of consciousness for two hours. I got up, stretched, and began to walk forward, dictating what I remembered into my little Pearlcorder.

I walked for many hours talking into my recorder. I didn't know if I was recording a dream or a past-life memory or a subconscious conglomeration of information I had at some time read in a history class when I was a child. Of one thing I was certain. I had never heard about anyone called John the Scot. It was only after the pilgrimage that I moved to research him. The information was difficult to find, but such a person did exist, according to one or two obscure textbooks, and he was a cleric-teacher in Charlemagne's court. As I researched the warfare along the Camino, only the battle of Roncesvalles was discussed. I did find reference to a giant Moor who had done hand-to-hand combat with the trusted and loyal soldier of Charlemagne's who was called Roland. He had become significant because he killed the giant. But more famous was the story of how Roland died, bringing up the rear guard of Charlemagne's army during the retreat at Roncesvalles, where Roland was killed for having sacked the city of Pamplona without Charlemagne's permission. The horn that Roland had blown for help was called Olifant.

The mythology, the history, my dream-vision that seemed to have been narrated by John the Scot, swirled in my head as

I walked. What was real? Who was Mike Flowers? Was this why so many people walked the Camino? Was it an internal history lesson of self as well as a physical experience?

✣ ✣ ✣

When I reached the next *refugio* in Los Arcos, I was exhausted. I remember it now as the "foot-massage *refugio*" because there was a man there who attended the pilgrims' feet for no charge. He said he understood the importance of feet because not only did they suffer but the energy of the Camino's ley lines permeated the meridians of the feet and into the energy system of the body, which was what gave the pilgrim the sense of self-realization. He claimed to receive a higher understanding himself from the energies he received from the massages. He had done the Camino many times and understood what every serious pilgrim was going through.

When I explained what had happened to me, he just nodded, unsurprised, and advised me not to question my sanity but to keep going, allowing whatever transpired to occur. It would all be clear in the end, he said. My conversation with him was a valuable gift because he assured me that, not all, but a good number of people had similar experiences if they were open to the reality of other dimensional truth. We had a discussion about the nature of human spiritual identity—who we were and who we might have been—and the possibility of other-

dimensional reality coming into focus as a result of the ampli-
fying of energy of the ground beneath us as we walked. He said
the Camino tested a pilgrim's capacity to love. He said the
ancients used it to balance masculine and feminine. "When the
yin and yang are merged, you have a divine understanding of
what you are in all dimensions," he said. "And as far as the feet
are concerned, the ancients used to walk with no shoes because
they understood that through the soles of the feet they could
find the knowledge of the soul." The "sole-soul" point of it all!
He went on to explain about the healing of reflexology, which
used pressure upon the meridian points of the feet to release
blocked energy and blocked memories. When the energy was
released, health resulted. "You could say," said the massage man,
"that health is also knowing your memories."

I was beginning to understand. I was now a spiritual
walker.

8

I spent a peaceful night in the *refugio*. When I woke, I saw a couple talking animatedly to each other. We introduced ourselves. The woman's name was Ali. She said she was from San Salvador. She was dressed for the Camino in a jumpsuit made by Gucci, carried a cosmetics bag made of leather, and wore double-decker sneakers purchased from a high-fashion mod shop somewhere. She had dark hair and dark eyes, carried another bag for hair curlers and an over-the-shoulder, expensive carryall. She was as amusing as her wardrobe. She was with a short, stocky man she introduced as Carlos.

"Carlos invited me to Spain to go on a promenade with him," she explained. "This is his idea of a casual walk around the manor?"

Carlos chuckled. He was a Basque, and even from his sharp body movements I could see he was defiant.

"She doesn't understand because she doesn't want to understand," he answered.

Ali threw up her hands in dramatic exasperation.

It turned out they had once been lovers about twenty-five years ago. But he got someone else pregnant and decided to marry her. Carrying a torch for Ali, some years later he invited her to come to Spain. I don't know if either of them really knew what they were doing on the Camino, but then, nobody did. They were a source of both amusement and irritation to me. Carlos was determined to carry out the task of completing the Camino as a serious pilgrim through sheer force of will. Ali, as I was to learn later, would often hail a bus when she got tired. Although she walked long hours before taking a bus, she (in her double-decker mod tennis shoes) never got one blister. Carlos argued that it was because she was frivolous and not serious; she said it was because she was lucky.

In any case, we began to walk together. That meant we were in sight of each other and only now and then did we carry on conversations. Usually we met up at the end of a ten-hour, twenty-five-kilometer (almost sixteen miles) trek, in the *refugio* of the next town or village. Carlos looked like a sunburned mountain climber in his Bermuda shorts and boots with red socks, with his tall stick, and authoritative, stocky, bowlegged stride. Ali somehow never broke a sweat even if she hadn't taken a bus.

It was some days before she admitted she was from a wealthy diplomatic family and lived in the San Fernando Valley in Los Angeles!

Carlos was a man of few words, mostly "No," "No," "No," to everything we did. Ali complained most of the time but tempered her complaints with hilarious, self-deprecating humor about how spoiled she was and what kind of appearance she must be creating in a *refugio,* where only the bare necessities were to be found, as she rolled her hair in curlers and rummaged through a makeup case made for a diva. Carlos rolled his eyes and unrolled his sleeping bag for Ali.

I supposed they were the entertainment I had created for myself in an environment where I didn't want to talk only to my stick.

So when Ali got tired and took a bus, Carlos gallantly asked if he could be of any help to me. Together, we walked through Torres del Río, Viana, Navarrete, Logroño, and Nájera, a distance of more than thirty miles.

In several towns the press attempted to accost me. Carlos interceded, and except for what was now a familiar picture, the newspapers had nothing to publish. I spoke to none of them, and by now the villagers were protecting me too. I would see them direct a reporter in the opposite direction as I hid behind a tree. Carlos enjoyed being the sergeant of my privacy, and I appreciated it.

In Santo Domingo, beyond Nájera, Ali pulled a muscle (still no blisters) and was forced to stay in a *refugio* for a few days while Carlos, who was as determined an overachiever as I, walked on just ahead of me.

I began to see large screws along the path every few hours. I didn't know if that meant I had a screw loose.

By now, about ten days into the trek, I had adjusted to the pain, tried to lean forward on my stick to eliminate uneven foot pressure, had met and talked to many strangers from all over the world, and tried to keep calm about the climate changes. I had my bag of homeopathy, which I dispensed to people in the *refugios* who were suffering from various maladies, and prayed that I would never have to interrupt the walk with a sprain or muscle spasm. When walking the flatlands, the temperature could be one hundred degrees. The hills were cooler and sometimes dropped to fifty degrees all in the same day. I had wanted to discard my Gortex jacket and slacks, but fortunately decided against that.

With Ali, Carlos, and sometimes new friends, I ate salad, wine, and bread at the end of every day. We could usually find a small restaurant not too far from the *refugio*. Sometimes when I lost them, I'd come into a village and, not speaking Castilian Spanish, have to wander for another few miles before I found a *refugio*. The Irish girls seemed always to be either a few days behind or a few days ahead of me. They always inquired about my press problems, and I said I'd be fine.

Then one morning in a *refugio* somewhere in one of the villages between Santo Domingo and Belorado, I was taking a cold shower (there was never hot water) when two photographers pulled back the curtain and began to take pictures. I slapped the cameras out of their hands, covered myself with the shower curtain, and screamed at them to leave. They did. I could see my press problem was going to be more and more difficult. I was most anxious not to trouble the other pilgrims with the baggage I brought along with my life, yet I knew if I held a press conference somewhere, the reporters would be more encouraged than ever. The Spanish press was relentless. A celebrity was not supposed to engage in a struggle like the Camino. They didn't understand. I could see why they were genuinely curious, but they had no sensitivity for what their own historic pilgrimage meant to people.

The other pilgrims were disturbed by the shower scene. I was mortified and quickly dressed and left by the back door.

I walked alone until I saw the yellow arrow and found myself on a busy highway. It was built over the old Camino. Three huge trucks bore down on me from behind. The wind of their passing nearly knocked me over. My new hat blew off into the stream of traffic, and I had to let it go. I couldn't stop and pull my old hat from my backpack, so I kept walking with the sun burning down on my face.

I tried to control my thoughts so that I wouldn't be afraid. I thought of movies, new ideas for my stage show, a leather purse I would buy when I got back to Madrid, the men I'd been with, my daughter. I didn't know what day it was. Well, at least I had lost ten pounds in ten days. What a diet!

Then I remembered what a great teacher had told me about fear: "Never ask yourself what it is you fear—instead, ask yourself what it is that concerns you. A fear thought, put out, will return, because all energy returns to the sender. Any energy always makes a loop until it regains the source. A concern thought will return also. At that moment discern why you're concerned."

I tried it. I thought to myself, "Why am I concerned right now at this moment?" Immediately, I had the answer. I was concerned that I might get hurt or die from a passing truck. I remembered all the times I had jokingly said, "Listen, if I get hit by a truck . . ." Those words might come home to roost on this Spanish highway. Very few pilgrims met such a fate, but I could see how it could happen.

Then I remembered. I had come to terms with dying before undertaking this pilgrimage.

Yes, I was prepared to die, if necessary.

Immediately, I had the next thought: Even if I left the body, I wouldn't die. On top of that, I remembered the dream-vision under the tree. It seemed that I was alive in another place and time and had a different body.

I began to relax as I trudged. Was dying just passing on to

another state of being until I decided to be born again? That was exactly what I believed. Now I was in a position to test that belief emotionally.

I relaxed more. The baking sun was burning my face, but the trucks didn't seem to come as close.

I began to think about how we each identify ourselves with our physical bodies more than our spirit. I knew in my heart that fundamentally I was a soul-being having a physical experience, not a fundamentally physical being whose soul would die upon "death." I *knew* that.

Why, before my spiritual search, had I thought of myself as basically physical? The Christian religion had taught me that. My religion claimed that souls had no preexistence. If my soul did not exist independent of my physical form, then according to the Christian religion, my human perspective was locked into my physical identity. I was born physical and struggled to become spiritual, rather than recognizing my true nature, which was that I was fundamentally a soul in the first place, choosing to have an experience in the physical.

My religion also said that my soul and body would join after resurrection and that I was therefore not complete without physicality. It said everything originates out of matter. I therefore developed an attachment not only to my body, which provided my identity, but also to material objects around me, which gave me social status and personal esteem in a physical world.

I could see how materialism was born. It came out of a dis-association with the soul and spirit. Materialism also caused a spiritual lethargy in human beings because we related much more to our physical surroundings than to our souls' needs.

Even our systems of government evolved from a disassoci-ation with spirit. Governments determined the flow of material wealth and goods and services and the control of nature, manip-ulating our survival resources and making decisions that should come from a spiritual recognition as much as an economic one. Economics and the manipulation of material resources (money, stock markets, bonds, banks, insurance companies, and so on) dic-tated whether one had an important participation in the deci-sions of a civilization and society. It was all determined according to what one had acquired and whether one was an important consumer. Therefore, materialism manipulated and determined the standard of values. That, in turn, informed the behavior of human beings.

There was nothing wrong with accumulating wealth or objects, or being body conscious, unless there was an addiction to it that eliminated the recognition of spirit. When one's very identity was invested in the physical and in acquisitions, it affected one's behavior and thus one's decisions in life.

The fear of losing one's wealth and one's body was the result of being disassociated from one's soul. And that fear lim-ited the growth of the soul, which was why we were here on earth in the first place. When the soul enters into matter and identifies more with matter than its original state of being, we have materialism. The church reinforced that identification by claiming there was no preexistence.

Here I was trudging along a highway that exemplified materialism, longing for a lighter backpack in a countryside that was poor, yet had more churches per capita than any other. I had wanted a revelation on the Camino? I was having a magnificent one!

9

I was now nearly halfway across northern Spain. I had made friends with people, found it easy to sleep in *refugios* and meld in with the other pilgrims, and was peaceful and contemplative when I walked. My body hurt, but I adjusted.

My "dream-visions" became more intense, sometimes to the point of alarming me, but only because they felt so real and I never liked the feeling that I had been unaware of or failed to recognize a truth.

Because of the press following me, I had felt not only invaded but also that I was in a race against time. I decided I would walk into Compostela on July 4. I would have done the Camino in thirty days. To me it would signify my liberation as an American.

Somehow my forty-day advice from my friend Anne Marie was forgotten, lost in the maze of evading the press and not wanting to disturb the search and motivation of the other pilgrims. I didn't want them burdened with my baggage, yet I was cognizant that I was also serving my overachievement compulsion.

I had not yet reached the abandoned village of Foncebadón, where the dog packs were, and the specter of that event was ever present in my mind. Perhaps what happened next was a precursor.

I was walking alone in the hills. Ali, Carlos, and the Irish were either days behind or days ahead. I was deep into a dream-vision about my past life as the Moorish girl. John the Scot was with me again, narrating the meaning of the pictures in my head.

I was in the court of Charlemagne, as before, poring over ancient manuscripts relating to the positions of the stars and their effect on human behavior. Charlemagne was a man who believed he should be able to control not only the tides, but also the stars. He was an insatiable conqueror for the sake of his pope. Together they would rule the destiny of the known world for Christ.

John the Scot was with us. Suddenly, John said to me, "Now, you wished to know the identity of your king in your present lifetime?"

"Yes," I answered.

"Look closely into his face. You will see."

I looked up into the conqueror's face. It began to change

until it formed the features of someone I knew. I was startled at my recognition. Then another voice overshadowed even the sight of his face as he spoke to me. "Yes," he said. "You are seeing me again."

It was the face and voice of Olaf Palme, the Swedish prime minister with whom I had had a love affair and whom I had written about in *Out on a Limb* and disguised as a British politician from the Labour party. "I have always wanted to change the world for the better," he said gently. "I tried to do it in the times I knew you. You inspired me, yet I couldn't accept you completely in either life because of the social implications."

Palme had been married when I was with him. He was assassinated by an unknown assailant, giving rise to swirling rumors that his killer had been a Moslem arms dealer. Palme had been a man of extraordinary intelligence and was instrumental in arbitrating the problems between the northern and southern countries (as he termed them) in the world. He was a socialist, but a strong proponent of democracy. If he had lived, he could have made a big difference in melding a socialist system of economics with democratic principles. He was married to a communist and believed that capitalism was running rampant but communism smothered free thought. He was sensitive, flexible, and yet believed one individual could effect tremendous change. The last time I saw him he told me that after his term as prime minister he would like the job of secretary general of the UN. If that occurred, he would be living in

New York and we would be able to spend more time together. I never pressed him on marriage because I wasn't certain I wanted that myself, but I was certain that he was a man I could have been happy with. We fit in every way, and he satisfied me intellectually and emotionally. There was one problem, however. He was paranoid about the press and very concerned about what our relationship would mean to his power. As karma would have it, he was assassinated as I was shooting the television film of *Out on a Limb* in Peru. At the moment he was killed, I was meeting with a Peruvian *brojo* (psychic). The *brojo* held objects in his hands that facilitated his clairvoyance. One of them was a small silver star. The star fell through his fingers. The *brojo* looked up at me and said, "Someone important to you has just passed on." I had no idea what he meant until I saw a Peruvian newspaper the next day, with all the details.

Now, as I sat against the huge wall fireplace and looked up at the king's face while we were discussing the stars, I felt a shiver run through me. John the Scot spoke. "You see, my child, you two have had a destiny together. If he had recognized your relationship in society's eyes in either incarnation, perhaps he could have effectuated his desires. Personal courage when one loves another is as important as the courage to effect change for the society. In the knowledge of who you are, you have the discipline and courage to carry out the agenda you set for yourself. He couldn't see his way clear to understanding that everything begins with self. Without an understanding of self and all that that entails, one cannot align oneself with the destiny chosen. His destiny had been to align the socialist states after their collapse. He could have aligned a new paradigm with socialism and freedom. He could have united socialist countries who desired personal freedom in a way that was workable."

I stared at the face of the king and almost laughed. This was too awe-inspiring, and yet it seemed to fit. Palme had had other women before me, and it hadn't troubled him. But then they were not interested in spiritual investigations. They were pure intellectuals. My spiritual leanings opened him to ridicule, and he gently tried to undermine my beliefs and questions at the same time that he understood there was something to them. I enjoyed the polarity, but I always felt I needed to warn him that he was out of touch with a fundamental truth that in the end would be his undoing. I never knew what I'd meant until now. When Palme died, I was devastated.

John continued. "The greatest form of love is to allow the consequences that accrue from another's own free will."

Yes, I understood that intellectually, but to absorb it emotionally was another matter.

The dream-vision vanished, and I walked on, thinking of synchronicity in the world. It seemed true that one could see it everywhere; every moment there was a reminder of the laws of cause and effect. I remembered that Palme, who believed in separation of church and state, had been responsible for eliminating prayer in the Swedish schools every morning and in doing so had, ironically, wiped out collective simultaneous meditation for Sweden's children (all of Sweden is in the same time zone). He had also been an atheist. Had he separated himself from the God Source and suffered the consequences?

If he had trusted the Swedish press with his personal life and confusions, would they have accepted it? I walked on, completely engrossed in my thoughts. I wasn't even aware that I was moving, when out of nowhere I found myself ambushed by a television crew and a woman reporter.

She shoved a microphone in front of my face.

I was so shocked it knocked the breath out of me, and then my shock turned to rage. I slammed the camera to the ground and then turned on the woman.

"What the hell do you want?" I demanded. She, unfazed, said, "Could you tell our audiences if you are becoming Catholic, and if not, why are you doing this Camino?"

Like a cornered animal, I shouted things at her that even my curse-proficient father couldn't have made up. I called her every combination of names in the book and ended with, "I hate you and everything you stand for."

The woman turned away from me, trying to hold back tears. Then I went after the camera crew, who were desperately attempting to record my outburst. I lunged toward them and they ran. That didn't stop me. I was relentless. I picked up a small boulder and, with my backpack thumping up and down, chased them up a mountainside. The woman stood below with tears on her cheeks and her mouth agape.

The three-man crew kept running from me. I kept chasing them. I couldn't believe what I was doing. I was an enraged fifteen-year-old going after the school bully. When I got to the top of the mountain, they were waiting for me. I knew the camera was on, but I didn't care. I threw the boulder at it, hoping it would be destroyed. It was, but another camera crew had been alerted somehow, and they got the film.

There was a small village at the top of the mountain. A hotel owner saw the scene in front of his place, shooed the crew away, and helped me into his hotel. My lungs were aching from the exertion, which took my breath away in the thin air. I couldn't speak. He led me to a private room, brought me tea, and after he determined that I was all right, left me alone.

What had just happened? The woman reporter was engaged in ambush journalism, but I believed she was also basically curious about why I was doing the Camino. On reflection, I felt sorry for her. I had decimated her with my words, even if she only understood half of what I was saying. I remembered that her tears came when I screamed, "I hate you."

The men, on the other hand, had laughed at me as I pursued them up the mountain, which was what egged me on. They knew I was twice as old as they were and had a backpack to boot. They also knew that if I was mad, it would make a better story.

I despised them for their insensitivity and would not stop until I hurt them somehow. I knew the last laugh would be theirs, as it usually is with the press, but I couldn't stop myself. Unfairness was something I'd go to the mat for. And I did. The film ran on television that night, but I was happy to see it was quite blurred.

I looked around the small room, saw a bed, and lay down on it. After a few minutes, John the Scot came to me.

"Well, lassie," he said to me. "The press-dogs certainly tested your temper, now, didn't they?"

"Yes," I answered sullenly.

"And you snarled back, didn't you?"

"Yes, I suppose so."

"Well, now, you were speaking their language, were you not?"

"Was I?" I asked.

"Most certainly," he answered. "They snarled in order to test your truth, much the way dogs do. You're afraid of the dogs up ahead, are you not?"

"Yes."

"Well, remember how you just handled the human version. Dogs have sensibilities they can't imagine that humans do *not* share. If you snarl, you will be speaking their language. When they snarl, it is an invitation to understand them. Dogs don't like it if you're dishonest with them. Neither does the press. They each nip at your heels until you face yourself. And if you have fear *combined* with malice, they will both consume you."

"Did I have malice against those press people?" I asked.

"No," he answered. "You had rage because they were unfair. Unfairness denotes an imbalance in life. The woman was hurt, but she must learn to ask her questions in a more fair way. You, child, could tend to your temper. But then you're Scots-Irish, are you not?"

"Yes," I answered, smiling to myself.

"Well, Scots-Irish are the masters of the Sorrows. They erupt because they feel deeply. I will explain more of the Scots-Irish character later, but for now, know the history of the dogs and the press along the Camino."

"What do you mean?" I asked, almost knowing that he was going to say something shocking.

"The souls you encountered today were soldiers in the ancient times who hounded and tortured people until they 'pressed' them to become Christians. They focused on the Moorish people, whom they regarded as infidels. They are still doing the same thing today. And some of the most cruel and torture-loving have returned as dogs; however, that fate is extremely rare. They return to haunt the same sites to test the honesty of humans. That is what you will find in Foncebadón. You have learned how to handle them today."

I didn't understand how snarling at them would protect me.

"You will see when you arrive there. The dogs and the press consider themselves masters of the truth."

I sighed and said nothing.

"One more thing," said John. "Your interest in Islam comes from your experience on the Camino as a Moorish girl. It is a good perspective from which to examine your concerns about Islamic fundamentalism in the world today."

John the Scot slipped away from my dream-vision. I lay there thinking about rabid dogs, rabid press, and rabid fundamentalism: Christian, Islamic, or otherwise.

The ancient hatreds between religions were a source of deep sorrow for me. I had read the prophecies that claimed Islam would cause great destruction in the world. From Nostradamus to Edgar Cayce to interpretations of Revelations in the Bible, the presence of Islam was associated with the end of the world as we know it. Was that possible? And if so, how?

Would the Moslem Albanians turn on the West at some time in the future? And since Islam was the fastest growing religion in the world, would there be a silent revolution from within the Christian countries? Would the Moslem countries unite against Israel and necessitate our coming to their aid, thereby precipitating Armageddon? Would, as some prophecies predicted, China and Iran unite and use nuclear weapons against the West?

Each religion seemed to have had its crusade. Were we going to experience the Moslem crusade in a way that would end the world as we know it?

Was all of the suffering in the world the result of karma that the human race perpetrated on itself? That was why we needed to go within ourselves to find our true identity through time. When we know who we are, we know the joys and sorrows of ourselves. When we admit that to ourselves, we can loosen the bonds of karma and move on.

As I was pondering these questions, lying on the bed, John came in again and gave me a dissertation on karma:

The fulfillment and resolution of the law of karma is the following: One drop of joy is so potent it will transform concern into compassion. That is the ability to give of yourself in the knowledge that whatever it is you give will return to you, improving your life and the lives of all those around you. One drop of joy plus courage becomes passion, which enables you to take effective action without thought. One drop of joy plus discipline becomes empathy, the ability to know that your emotions are real and all those around you are real, which then restores your God-consciousness. When you realize the energetics of all things, you understand that God resides in all things. This, then, is the unification of the upper and lower chakras, where you marry the masculine and the feminine in yourself—the God and Goddess within yourself.

The law of karma is not the return of events, but more the return to your soul. As you come into the God realization, your ability to move through everything is restored. Your inability to move is the definition of sorrow. When you empty yourself out of sorrow, you enable yourself to receive the next level of joy.

The Holy Grail is an example. It is like any other cup except that its real value lies in its emptiness. The joy comes when the cup of sorrow is emptied. Therefore, the joys of the sorrows along the Camino are the rediscovery of your own soul. . . . Mankind, therefore, has a moral duty to seek joy.

John vanished in my head, and I recorded what he said as best I could.

I then lay back and thought about it.

I felt the courage to go forward was located in a place in my heart. I could feel it physically. The feeling of courage did not reside in my mind. It was a heart feeling that said I had the knowledge that I had the mind, body, and spirit to do anything. And the courage enabled me to move forward by going within.

I thought of a house that was burning with me inside it. The only way out was through the flames. I was experiencing the journey through the flames. A primary emotion was the ability to feel concern. Whenever I felt concern and didn't act on it, I became angry. If I had the resolve to go within, I could transform the anger into courage and thus move forward.

The people in the cars along the highway who yelled *"Ultreya!"* were giving me the courage to go within. So the real discipline was not the focus of will to the exclusion of everything else, but more the ability to look inside myself and receive what already belonged to me—JOY.

I thought of dashing up the mountain after the camera crew. The mountain had been a focus of my angry will.

Symbolically, everything from a mountain ultimately crumbles to the valley floor. Everything flows to a valley. All I needed to do was become a valley in order to receive what already belonged to me. In other words, surrender—surrender to the knowledge that within myself was the balance of masculine and feminine and the ability to find joy in whatever occurred. All of life was a lesson in self-knowledge. The more knowledge we have of ourselves, the more we are able to deal with anything.

Our leaders in the world today were examples of that. Each of them was suffering from a lack of self-knowledge. That was why so many of them acted in ways that were destructive. They were, in effect, *self*-destructive, not only of themselves but of the people they led—Clinton, Milosevic, Osama bin Laden, the mullahs in Iran, the leaders in China, and so on. The leaders I had known who spent time in prison in solitary confinement—Gandhi, Nelson Mandela—had resolved so many of their inner conflicts because they had had isolation forced upon them. And they all said that was the most important time of their lives. Today, not many took the time for the inner search, hence the state of the world, which bordered on the brink of disaster. Certainly, the regular people in any given society had no time for the inner search because they were caught up in the competition of survival, due to rampant materialism. The people of the world seemed to be on a treadmill of survival, ignoring the joys of evolution, which could only come from taking the time to know who they were.

I didn't want that to continue to happen to me any longer. It was as the poet Yeats had said, "The only journey worth taking is the journey within." If the journey within revealed that I had been many people in many different times, then so be it. At least I would have the equipment with which to evaluate how to fulfill the personal destiny I had been born to.

10

As I reached the halfway point on the Camino, I noticed the *refugios* were less full. Had people begun to drop out?

People were more harsh, less respectful of each other, and more aggressive.

Three drunks followed me out of a bar where I had bought orange juice. I turned and just stared at them. They went away. Some young girls ran after me for autographs. I signed and gently moved on.

It was difficult to hear on the streets of the cities I crossed; so much din from cars, conversations, and arguments.

My hands were cracked and red, my face peeling from the sunburn, and the backpack felt as though it weighed a ton. Yes, it was better to walk with nothing.

If I ate in the morning, I was hungry all day. So I didn't eat yogurt and nuts and fruit until the afternoons. The villages and towns were shuttered for siesta anyway.

The fountains in each village were always quaint and inviting. I'd fill my water bottle, knowing I would be water-safe until the next one.

Ali started taking buses frequently, and Carlos became difficult. At one point I asked Ali to take my backpack for me to the next village. I immediately began to stumble, was uncentered, and lost my balance with no weight on my back. I had no control over my ability to walk and found it curiously difficult to go on. With the burden of my backpack lifted, I felt the freedom to allow myself to feel anger at some of the people in my life. There were unresolved issues with them, as well as in my family, and I allowed myself to look at some of them. I found myself realizing how I had contributed to those conflicts. And then I realized that each person had been a mirror and teacher for me to know myself better. That was what family members did for each other. That was why families were the formal education for each member before entering into the world. And I believed each member *chose to be born* into the family to serve the others. I would try to remember that whenever an argument fraught with emotion and uncommunicated feelings happened when I returned home.

The farmers along the way talked with discouragement over the price of wheat and the lack of rain.

I could feel the energy field of the Camino as I walked

from Belorado on to Villafranca. Butterflies surrounded me. They were purple and pink and white and black and orange and yellow. I thought how they had previously crawled as caterpillars before becoming free and so exquisite. *They* were joyous and contributed beauty to all who thrilled to them. I still felt like a caterpillar. When would I become a butterfly?

I walked about twenty-two miles a day. I could feel a gentle magic occurring, almost too gentle to realize. The press seemed to be tiring of following me. One photographer took a picture of me hanging up my clothes and departed.

I revamped my show as I walked; I designed a perimeter fence for my ranch and thought of new ways to obtain financing for character-driven films, which were so hard to get greenlighted. I would spend some money on a remodeled bedroom and maybe do a small show on Broadway. Underneath all my thoughts about my life in the world back home was the new world inside myself.

A man in a wheelchair sped past me going about twenty-five miles an hour. He was paralyzed, and I came to see later that he depended on people in the *refugios* to take care of his needs. Sometimes they did and sometimes they ignored him. I wondered what his karma was.

I met a woman named Baby Consuelo, whom I'd met in Brazil years before. She was a singer and did just that as she walked. She was much faster than I, and I never saw her again until the last day.

Then I came into San Juan de Ortega and realized why the press had seemed to dissipate along the Camino.

There were two hundred of them waiting for me at the church. Ali and Carlos were waiting there too. Carlos came to meet me and told me that the priest had offered the journalists an interview with me in return for a donation to his church. I told Carlos to tell them I didn't think it was fair. He readily accommodated and told them off, including the priest.

The priest offered me garlic soup, which I refused and continued on my way.

Somewhere outside of town I lay down under a tree and fell asleep with my hat over my face.

John the Scot came in. He told me that I had known some of the priests in my days as the Moorish girl. He said they were innkeepers in those days. They traveled up and down the trail gossiping. They provided meals and entertainment for pilgrims. Then they took to selling religious artifacts, which they claimed would protect the pilgrims. The pilgrims paid exorbitant prices for artifacts that were worth nothing, but they were too embarrassed to turn them down. Those innkeepers were priests today!

He said I had known Carlos and Ali along the trail. Ali had been a Moor who authentically converted to the Christian religion. She had lost her parents during the conflicts, and he, John, had taken her in and given her sanctuary. I had helped her reach

France, where she became Carlos's ward. He gave her some land. He fell in love with her then too, but his duties to the Christians forbade him the consummation of that relationship. They remained dutiful to each other, and as everyone returns to old haunts, they came together in this lifetime again.

Then John said, "You have a theme here which you must be noticing. It is the theme of lovers not loving deeply enough because of powerful prejudices. Those prejudices tainted the ability of each lover to reach completion in himself . . . including you." That had been true with the king and again with Palme.

John went on to say that the man in the wheelchair was in an extended episode of madness. He had been a cripple in each lifetime and had vowed to continue his dedication to his malady every century. John said he was a Christian version of a Buddhist monk who believed suffering was the path to God and that it also amplified the compassion of others. This repeating of a lifetime experience was a little like the situation of the Dalai Lama, always coming back to do the same thing, like reading an important book over and over.

He said Carlos had desired a unification of the sacred trails both in France and in Spain under the protection of the Knights Templar.

He said that Anna had been a tutor of mine when I was very young in the land of the Moors, and she was reenacting that same role for me now.

He told me that Mme. de Brill, the awful woman at the beginning in Saint-Jean-Pied-de-Port was what he called a sin eater. "She eats other people's sins so that the Camino will be easier for them. She is the gatekeeper at the border between France and Spain. She has been doing this for centuries. That is the reason for her negative attitude. She takes on other people's sins."

John ended with telling me I would have a disturbing encounter with someone in a *refugio* some days ahead and I should react as I wanted, but he would explain the reason for it later.

I could see that John the Scot was my real guide along the Camino. He had done the same for me in the past. I couldn't explain how it worked or why. I was to learn that later too.

✠ ✠ ✠

In Burgos, a man approached me with the gift of a new staff. It had a ring of silver around the top and the bottom. I hesitated. I didn't want to give up my old friend.

The man led me to a very well laid out *refugio* with a dining room. He had prepared food for the pilgrims who had arrived there that day. I was now wary. I didn't want to be impolite, but I wondered what the catch was.

Carlos and Ali trailed in, and we sat down to eat. The garlic soup was more oily than usual, the bread three days old, the wine sour. There were cans of sardines, which we had to dig out with knives because there were no forks. I wondered if this was a joke.

The man hovered as he watched us eat. I couldn't do it. I finally said I couldn't eat during the day. He frowned.

I had a decision to make about the new staff. My old one was like a sorcerer's crooked stick. So familiar had it become that to walk with it was like walking with my kindly grandfather. But I knew the new one would be better for my back because it was strong and straight. Ali, as yet, didn't use a staff. Carlos had one of his own.

I stood from the table, walked with both staffs for a moment, and made a decision. I would give my old staff to the priest of the previous town. Perhaps he could use a trusted friend, but I didn't want to retrace my steps to his church.

I heard a commotion and looked outside. Another group of press people had gathered, and beside them was the priest. I walked outside and presented him with my old stick. He turned it upside down, bent it, laughed, and discarded it. It made me angry that he didn't respect what a friend it had been to me. Carlos sidled up to me. "He is dishonest inside."

I didn't stop for questions or pictures and walked on, leaving my old friend, the sorcerer's stick, behind. It was hard for me to do. I had emotional attachments to many things, always wondering if I would need them in the future. Then I remembered a dream I had had once. I was the keeper of the records in some vast library of scrolls. I would often lend out the scrolls to people who wanted to study them. When the high commissioner of the library asked me for a detailed record of my inventory, most of the scrolls were not there. He was very angry. I vowed that would never happen to me again.

Now, I walked with my new staff, thinking about my relationship to things and how I would feel if I were a true refugee who had nothing. On one hand, I would feel liberated; on the other, I would feel deprived. Life on earth lay somewhere in the middle—the middle way, as the Buddhists said, comparing the concept to a harp string. If it is strung too tight, it won't play; if it is too loose, it hangs. The tension that produces the beautiful sound lies in the middle.

I wore my hat at all times now because the roots of my colored hair were growing out and I was embarrassed.

Ali and Carlos argued about his wife. They overlapped each other when they argued . . . something about his wife being fat and nobody likes fat people. Carlos was autocratic with Ali and she was petulant. Ali said she had forgotten her watch and ran back to the *refugio* to retrieve it. She returned later to say it had been in her bag all along. As I left a *refugio* every morning, I was also afraid I would leave something necessary behind.

Huge raindrops began to fall. I saw an isolated phone booth. I called my friend Anne Marie in California. She said she had played a previous message of mine for my daughter, Sachi. She said Sachi had cried because she didn't understand why I was doing this. Sachi never understood me or the search I was on. Well, I thought, who could understand it?

A squall came up. I put on my yellow poncho. The Camino was now pitted with holes and crevices and stones that shifted under my feet. The smell of sweat and dust was accentuated by the raindrops and wind. I had no spatial understanding of my backpack in the wind and rain. It blew from side to side. I tottered off my center, but loved the feeling of being safe under my waterproofed poncho. I slid down hillsides and worried about missing the yellow arrows. Ali had a Gucci-designed poncho over her, while her double-decker Maxfield's tennis shoes collected mud up to her ankles. Carlos strode forward with his Basque determination, making me giggle. None of us fell. There would be no press for a while.

A few hours later we stumbled into a small bar. I didn't know where we were. The bar was crammed with men, smoking and yelling at the ever-present bicycle races on TV. I couldn't hear myself think. The proprietress brought us coffee. Ali looked into her cup and screamed. There was a fly in it. She was horrified. Carlos commanded her to say nothing, reached in, removed the fly, and put it on the counter. The proprietress was mortified and gave Ali a fresh cup.

A conversation then ensued with Carlos and Ali discussing the "common" people. I couldn't decide who was taking which side. Carlos seemed imperious, and Ali personally affronted. Carlos said he couldn't bear the behavior of common people. I then launched into a description of my trip in 1973 to China, where the imperial elite like him were sent down to the communes to learn the wonder and glory of growing a tomato. He said, "Well, there's something positive in everything."

Ali then piped up, "Well, I didn't come all this way to make a promenade, then find it so grueling, and *then* end up with a fly in my coffee."

"No," said Carlos, "you were careless not to see the fly in your coffee."

"No," said Ali, "the proprietress was careless not to see it was there when she served it to me."

I was confused. The fly was on the counter, and Ali had a fresh cup.

Carlos then said, "You drink the coffee, the fly is in it, and down it goes."

"No," she responded. "No, *not* down it goes. And that is the difference between you and me." Then she gagged and blamed it on the fly and said she was sick.

The fly was in the trash by now, but that didn't stop them.

"I was freezing in the *refugio* last night, but I would rather have died than place the blanket from the shelter over me."

"Yes, well," said Carlos, "I gave you my sleeping bag. You refused that too. So you were cold."

"Everything around me is unclean," Ali went on.

"It's not so bad," said Carlos. "You must learn to be one of the people and not so spoiled."

I was really confused now. Neither liked the "common" people, but that must have been a good excuse for arguing.

The fly-and-common-people argument went on for an hour. Perhaps they should have married. I felt myself silently point my finger at them with the other three pointing to myself.

I walked outside. The squalls were over. The peaceful stillness belied that the storm had ever happened.

* * *

I now had blisters upon blisters. I needed to puncture them and sew them up. I needed to take a hot shower. I needed to be alone in a bedroom. I needed to feel my hair clean. I needed to look in a mirror. I needed to rearrange my tapes and determine if they were even recording. Somewhere in Burgos I found a hotel and checked in. Ali and Carlos, determined to be one of the common people, said they would find a *refugio*. I remembered a remark the playwright Clifford Odets had made to me as he lay dying. "You have no idea how much pleasure there is in things no larger than a fly's eye."

In the luxury of a small hotel room, I washed all my clothes in hot water, took a long, hot shower with real soap, washed my hair with real shampoo, sat on a private toilet, and tended to my blisters. I realized they were so bad because my weight had shifted while using the new staff. Then I had an interesting

thought: Wisdom was represented by what we stood upon—
our feet. That was why saints had their feet washed by others
who were in the early stages of enlightenment. The feet took
energy from the wisdom of Mother Earth and put us in touch
with our own balance. Did the saints ever take an oxcart when
they walked the Camino? Would taking a bus represent the
modern version of an oxcart?

I thought about the fact that I was born under the sign of
Taurus. I was an earth sign. An astrologer had told me that Taurus people like to run with ankle weights on because they are
fixed earth people. A Taurus has earth-based wisdom, while still
commanding the issues of love, beauty, and sensuality, because
Taurus is ruled by Venus. I came into this lifetime as a Taurus,
born at the end of April, to deal with the issues of physical love
and balancing the energies of masculine and feminine. Taurus
was the most dense of the signs, which meant I wanted to experience the primal identity after incarnating into the earth plane.
I elected a difficult physical life because I was a Taurus. *And* I
was a Scots-Irish Taurus. John the Scot had said the Scots-Irish
were the masters of the Sorrows. What did he mean? We were
certainly mad and riotous. Was that to deflect the sorrow? And
on what was the sorrow based? I shouldn't confuse sorrow with
depression. They were very different feelings.

I lay back in the privacy of my soft bed with actual clean
sheets and fell asleep. John the Scot didn't visit me. Instead, I had
my recurring dream about the gorilla. The monstrous gorilla was

chasing me. He chased me around the world, in various countries, up and down mountains, over hill and dale, until finally I found myself at the edge of the world. I knew I would either have to jump over the precipice in order to escape him or turn around and confront him. I chose to confront. I looked into his eyes and said, "What should I do now?" He answered me, "I don't know, it's *your* dream."

Was life my gorilla? And was it saying to me, "It's your dream. Do what you want with it"?

11

Through San Juan de Ortega, the city of Burgos, Castrojeriz, Frómista, Carrión de los Condes, and on, to Sahagún I walked, sometimes with people, sometimes alone. There were beautiful and refreshing fountains in each village, where I stopped to drink, think, and enjoy. As if on purpose, John the Scot didn't visit me. I was on my own with my understanding. Ali and Carlos were now on their own pace too, away from me. I wondered when I would say good-bye to them for good. I always had a problem leaving people. I felt guilty about leaving people behind. I knew we all had our own journey, but part of being successful was being out in front and leaving others behind. I noticed that the wealthy pilgrims always moved faster because they were more goal-oriented.

They didn't seem to *become* the Camino, or the path beneath their feet or the countryside or the sky or the flowers and wheat and clouds. They never seemed lost in the moment.

Some of the pilgrims said they could tell whether I was staying in a shelter or not by my familiar clothes hanging on the line outside.

A doctor tended to my blisters, and I tried to give him a thousand pesetas. He wouldn't take the money. Instead, he went away and came back with flowers for me. "When one walks for God, they shouldn't be charged," he said. "They should be rewarded."

I approached a wooden obelisk just outside of a small village. Carved into it was ULTREYA.

*   *   *

The city of Burgos was saturated with history and art. At the entrance to it, outside the walls, stood the ancient remains of the Hospital de San Juan Evangelista, and adjacent to it was a silent and comforting Benedictine monastery. I crossed a moat by a tiny medieval bridge and found myself in a medieval city. Here, in the grand cathedral that dates back to the thirteenth and fourteenth centuries, lies the tomb of the legendary El Cid. I reveled in the antiquity of this magnificent Gothic structure, thinking I had probably been here centuries before that!

Between Burgos and Castrojeriz, I crossed territory that is

famous for being one of the most difficult stretches on the Camino. I climbed the hills steadily, crossing the upper part of a stream coming from the Corrales de la Nuez, which were farmsteads, and reached the height of the first meseta, the dry Spanish plains, very like a desert of wheat fields and very poor.

I was suddenly into my next level of tolerance.

Mosquitoes and other insects dive-bombed me. I had my mosquito netting in my backpack, but it all happened so fast I was too late. As I stopped and unzipped my backpack, my face became a human feast. They were in my hair, my eyes, my ears, all over my hands, and diving against my leggings and shoes.

I thought of the night I spent lying in the sarcophagus of the King's Chamber in the Great Pyramid at Giza. It was legendary that if you lay in the sarcophagus, you would manifest that which you needed to clear and resolve. One of my points of unresolution was mosquitoes. I couldn't bear them. Sometimes when I was with others, the mosquitoes bothered only *me*. I drew to me what I was afraid of. There, as I lay in the sarcophagus, I was suddenly covered with them. They came from nowhere. I lay there meditating for them to go away. But my attitude toward them was based on fear, and they wouldn't leave. I had not yet learned to ask why I was concerned, not why I was afraid. It had been a miserable night, alleviated only by a citronella candle I had brought.

Now I was having the same problem. The mosquitoes swarmed around me as I finally secured the netting around my head—with none trapped inside, thank God. I watched them as they tried to eat through my shirtsleeves and leggings. It was good to be inside my net cage as I walked faster. Again I thought, Why am I concerned? It was because I didn't want to die from being bitten. I knew that was ridiculous. But I also didn't like the idea of them sucking my blood. I laughed to myself. Maybe that came from a vampire past-life experience.

A little further on, I came across two German men. They were not bothered by the mosquitoes. They said they had walked forty-eight kilometers (almost thirty miles) that day. One of them was about to be a father, and he was deciding whether to marry the mother while on the Camino. He said that if he didn't marry and something happened to the mother, under German law the state would take the baby away and place it in an orphanage. The other German was having so many relationships with both men and women he was walking to figure himself out.

We talked of commitment and of blisters and of wool versus cotton versus capoline until my mosquitoes went to feed elsewhere. I walked on by myself.

Twenty miles later I arrived at Frómista, where John's prophecy came true.

The *refugio* was pleasant enough, with a yard in the back and a nice clothesline. I washed one set of T-shirts and hung them out to dry overnight; then I cleaned my boots and carefully placed them under a bunk I chose. There was no one else in the *refugio*.

Suddenly, a woman came around the corner shrieking that

there were clothes on the line. She ripped them off and flung them to the ground and began to berate me for reasons I didn't understand. I didn't know who she was or whether she had anything to do with the shelter. I gathered up my wet clothes and folded them, put them on my cot and sat down. She stood over me and screamed again. I didn't know what to do. A couple came in. She screamed at them. They turned around and left. I sat on my bunk listening to the woman go insane. Her eyes were those of a wild dog. I stood up, trying to understand. What did this mean? She turned to the walls, and shrieking at them, she left.

I was shaking. I began to cry. I felt totally alone in an insane world. I could cope with most anything if I understood it. But insanity was not logical. I wiped my tears. I needed to get hold of myself. I undressed, put my small towel in front of me, and then found a shower. Perhaps the cold water would help. As I drained my tensions under the cold water, the shower curtain opened and a photographer stepped into the shower. He popped his flash-bulbs in my face, taking pictures. I flailed at him until his camera dropped from his hands into the water. Yelling in what little Spanish I knew, I told him to go away. There were other photographers outside. I yelled at them until they disappeared. Still shaking, I dried myself, dressed, and walked outside. No one was there. Had I made all this up? I was wearing a light pair of thong shoes, but my feet hurt so much I could hardly move. My arms felt like lead poles. I had my money belt with credit cards around my waist. I made my way into the village. I spotted a phone booth and placed a credit card call to my friends at my ranch in New Mexico. When they answered, I felt safe for a moment just hearing their voices. Then I heard a TV set loudly playing in the background. I heard the excited voice of a television reporter who was apparently following a car chase on the freeways of Los Angeles. Someone had murdered his wife and was escaping to Mexico. It was O. J. Simpson, and his wife and a friend of hers had had their throats cut. Was I in the real world? And which was crazier—the Spanish *refugio* or the City of the Angels?

* * *

The next morning I headed into real meseta country alone. Ali and Carlos hadn't made it to Frómista. The road was dotted with loose pebbles, so my entertainment was to maneuver around two stones that had plopped into my shoes. It took so much energy to stop and remove them, so I played a game rolling them around with my toes so they wouldn't cause more blisters. A wind came up. I stopped and removed the pebbles, secured my hat, and pressed on. In no time, more stones were in my shoes. I couldn't figure out how they got there. Through the wind I tried to focus on which stones would jump over my boots and fulfill their seeming destiny to cause blisters. The wind blew dust into my face.

I had friends in the States who were involved with the Hopi Indian tribe. The Hopis said that from the last decade of the twentieth century and after the turn of the millennium, it would be necessary for man to "tie himself to a tree." In other words, "big wind." They said the weather would become unpredictable and would "cleanse away many things with wind and rain." They said we must each be self-sustained and go back to growing our food from Mother Earth. Above all, they said, man needed to go within himself in order to gain spiritual understanding of what would be happening.

Their prophecies matched the Mayan prophecies. From what I saw occurring with the weather, they seemed quite accurate.

As I walked, I saw squadrons of storks. They made their nests among high trees and atop church steeples in the villages. Packs of dogs congregated under them. The wind stopped.

Bees, butterflies, birds, and some mosquitoes fluttered up against the sky and fields that stretched as far as I could see. A porcupine lay dead, killed while crossing the road. I could certainly understand that. My upper body was very sore as a result of the weight shift with my new staff. I hadn't named this staff either. My angel Ariel hadn't been around for weeks. John the Scot seemed to have replaced the vanilla-scented angel. But he wasn't around either. I walked as though in a trance, a moving meditation on my life and times. It was impossible to get away from myself. I was all I had. My legs began seriously to hurt. I could see why people quit. In fact, at this point many people did. I saw discarded shoes, trousers, shirts, and books along the way. I wondered if anyone ever cleaned the Camino.

Whenever I thought it was so hot I couldn't take another step, a breeze churned around me. A gift from God, somehow. If I was going to make Compostela by July 4, I'd have to double up on my pace. I did just that. I was certainly my mother's daughter. She would set her mind to a task, and nothing or no one could divert her. She walked past her benches all the time. I used to watch her put herself in a trance state of determination until she accomplished her task, regardless of the diversions or the consequences. I had begun emulating her by the time I was ten years old. Many times into my adulthood I found myself exhibiting her traits of determination, to the point where, ironically, it shocked her. Many times she remarked aloud at my drive and refusal to give up. And she wondered where it came from! She would shake her head in noncomprehension.

A Belgian hiker stopped me and said I had been his older sister in a past life. It was probably true. He was carrying a baseball bat and some larger contraption that he said would paralyze any dogs or people who might attack him. He wanted to talk about God and the universe and the meaning of life. I didn't. I wanted silence. I told him it was better to walk alone quietly. He asked me to bless him. That made me extremely uncomfortable. I didn't like being seen as a New Age guru. That was the reason I quit conducting my traveling seminars. Too many people gave their power away to me. *I* wasn't the reason they got something out of them; *they* were their own reason. And when people began to follow me to other cities, I knew it was time to stop. I didn't really know any more than anyone else anyway. I couldn't even explain why I was doing this pilgrimage except to take a journey through myself.

*   *   *

I was now on a mountain trail when suddenly I came to a dead end. The path went no further. I couldn't find any yellow arrows. I was lost again. I retraced my steps for about five hours until I reached a bridge that was down. I didn't know which way to go. I heard some cars, so I followed the sound until I reached a lone highway. I walked along the highway for another few hours, looking for the yellow arrows. It began to pour. I pulled out my Gortex jacket and plastic poncho. It was chilly.

Someone in a car stopped. "The arrows wrong," he said in Spanglish. "The bridge down for few months. Nobody fix."

"Which way do I go, then?" I asked. He pointed west, of course, along the highway. I was going west. *"Ultreya,"* he shouted as his car disappeared.

I clutched my poncho around me and walked some more. Finally, I saw a yellow arrow that led into the hills. I followed. I was now out of water with no way to catch the rain. I walked on until I found myself in what looked like a military installation. Two soldiers stopped me. "Not allowed," they said. "Not allowed further. Arrows you follow two years old."

Oh, God, I thought. Now I was really stuck. I walked away

from them, retracing my steps, and I was very thirsty. I had been walking since six A.M. It was now six P.M.

Two young girls approached me with a bottle of water and a bunch of flowers. I saw a small doll-like house nestled in the trees. They smiled and handed me the flowers. "We see your picture—*ultreya*." They stepped aside and pointed to the road again.

I walked in that direction. I had to get to a *refugio* before dark, and I didn't even know which or where the next village was. When the girls were out of sight, I stopped and sat down to pee. I sat in an anthill. The ants crawled up my legs and stung me. I poured precious water from the bottle and drowned them, and walked on.

I would not be afraid. I was at a dinner party in New York. Then I was swimming in the Pacific. I was in a trailer between setups on a movie set. I was performing on a stage. I concocted a blurred tapestry of activities in my mind's eye.

I passed four more screws on the path. I really was terribly lost. I didn't know what to do. For some reason I thought of how my father would have laughed at the four screws on the path. "You're really screwed this time," he would have said. And then suddenly, I felt him near me. Of course, he was not there, but I felt that his energy was. Then, next to him was Mother. They didn't say anything. They just comforted me. Then I felt them propel me to an alternative, almost obscure path. I followed it. They seemed to be walking beside me. I felt they had come together for the first time since both had passed on. I very strongly felt they had come together on the other side to guide me. My eyes welled up. Then I saw a road. I was a mess of emotion by now. I wanted to talk to them, ask how they were. What was it like over there? But a truck stopped. The man inside offered me a ride. I thanked him, refused, and he nodded, seeming to understand. He pointed me to the next village, said there was a correct arrow a little further up the road. I focused again on Mom and Dad. But they were gone. . . . They had been there for me when they were alive and had done the same now.

I found the arrow and walked for a few more hours, thinking of how my parents had devoted their lives to their children while sacrificing their own dreams. I wondered what my own life would be like if they hadn't. And then, grateful, I came to a village and a *refugio*.

I slept without dinner, only water, remembering my mother and father. I felt them smiling down on me.

12

The next day was entirely different. Each village blurred into the next. I was somewhere in the state of Palencia. I walked alone again.

Bright sun was followed by driving rain. Double rainbows appeared over me, spurring me on. I walked through their colors as they met the ground. I breathed in the purple and red and orange and yellow. I breathed in the air, ran it through my brain cells and breathed out again. My brain and consciousness became the rainbows. I thought of the colors of the rainbows and how they matched the colors of the esoteric energy systems in the human body. Not too many people in the West understood or had even heard of the chakra system within us.

There are seven chakras, and each is a center of energy through which we literally derive our balance and consciousness. The Hindus and Buddhists were very familiar with the importance of the chakras, but this essential knowledge had not yet been widely accepted in the New World. Each chakra has a color and is associated with issues of living. For example, the base chakra, located at the root of the spine, is where we energetically experience fight or flight. It is the color red. Going upward slightly, the next energy center is orange and deals with creativity and sexuality. The third is yellow and deals with personal power. The fourth, green, is the heart chakra, through which we experience love; the fifth, blue, is located in the throat and deals with personal expression; the sixth, indigo, is the chakra of vision; and the seventh, violet, is the spiritual center at the top of the head.

As I looked up at the rainbows, I was reminded once again that these colors corresponded exactly to the inner colors of the human chakra system. We were each our own rainbow. In sophisticated spiritual circles, people do their chakra balancing every morning because they understand it is necessary for happiness. A bad mood can come from an unbalanced chakra, and by meditating on the color of each one's location, you can alter the energy that accompanies a bad mood.

I breathed in and visualized each color of the rainbow streaming through my own chakra system. Everything I needed was contained in these colors. That's how the Buddhist monks reached their bliss.

Slowly the pain left my legs and feet. My shoulders relaxed, and I actually started to skip. The backpack became almost weightless. I found myself walking on the balls of my feet first, not the heels. I remembered seeing the lamas in the Himalayas float down the mountainsides in the same fashion. They touched the hillsides with the balls of their feet so lightly that they looked as though they were floating. I saw lamas immerse themselves in ice water, and when meditating, steam rose from their bodies. They knew the value of visualized energy. It was more power-ful than the physical. It actually informed the physical. They knew that consciousness was energy. And that was why Tibetan medicine was so effective. It activated the chi (life force) in each chakra center and healed the body.

The trees on the mountainside seemed to be dancing to the music of the wind. It was my favorite kind of orchestral per-formance. A storm cloud would thunder a percussion. Then lightning crashed like cymbals, and a rain of what sounded like violas and cellos and whistling flutes enveloped me. I opened my Gortex jacket and ripped off my poncho. I didn't want pro-tection from my orchestra.

I smelled the ozone in the air, knowing that it heralded more lightning flashes.

I was utterly happy and part of everything around me. I stretched out my arms, welcoming the raindrops, and began to turn around and around. The thunder timpani rumbled in rhythm to my turns until the cymbal lightning crash accented my stop in mid-turn. I looked up and saw the sun shimmering above the storm. I felt warmth in my eyes. And when I gazed up at the reflection of the sun on the rain, I saw that there were two more arched rainbows above the storm. Then the percussion of clouds cleared, the violins of breeze washed away the drama of water music, and there was sheer silence. The trees swayed and bowed in appreciation as though they had adored the spectacle they had been a part of. I felt that I had been the conductor.

*   *   *

The *refugio* at the end of such a magical day was disgusting, as though God was reminding me there was always a duality.

Trash, dust, and filth covered the floor. The smell was vile. I didn't know where I was, and it didn't matter. I placed my sleeping bag on a cot that had been eaten away by rats, then unzipped it, and careful not to touch anything, I eased myself inside. I was oblivious of the snores and coughing of the homeless travelers around me, who were too exhausted to notice the conditions. I blew my nose on a precious piece of Kleenex and kept it beside me, knowing that I could use it for the toilet in the morning. A mere plastic bag or a piece of tissue could be as valuable as gold when you learn to carry nothing with you. I fell asleep listening to the rats scurrying along the floor, hoping they wouldn't make it up the side of my cot.

I had a dream that night that I had gone to heaven, which was inside an airport. My parents were there to meet me. My father stood straight and curious as I descended from some kind of flying machine. I looked around for Mother. She was huddled up against the walls of heaven. I couldn't interpret that dream then, but I believe I might have some understanding now. My father had lived his life in a pathless way. He noticed everything along the road. Time never meant much to him, which was why he was essentially an underachiever. Mother always looked to the end of the path for her children, desiring us just to get there. He would have understood my appreciation of the storm. She would have said, "Walk faster and come home successfully." Even though I was more a creature of my mother's goals, I was trying to balance the two. The process, the path itself, was the fulfillment and the achievement.

✳   ✳   ✳

Ali and Carlos arrived late in the night. Ali had bad shinsplints and refused to sleep in the filth of the *refugio*. I turned over and went back to sleep.

When I awoke, Carlos was sweeping the place himself. Ali watched and took another Advil. She was on a diet of Advil, wine, and tranquilizers by now. However, she still had no blisters.

We were joined by an Englishwoman who opined that she had to go back and support her husband in England. Somehow this led to a discussion about infidelity. She said that she had absolutely never been unfaithful to her husband. I then turned to Carlos and spontaneously asked him if he had ever been unfaithful to his wife. He smiled and answered, "In twenty-six years, never." I asked why he was smiling. He answered, "Because you even presumed to ask the question."

Ali, of course, rolled her eyes. She didn't believe him. I wasn't sure. The Englishwoman suddenly screamed. We all turned to see what was wrong.

"I've lost my wedding ring," she said.

I smelled my clothes and promised I would burn them at the end of the journey.

✳   ✳   ✳

I was now into the third week, and the trek between Carrión de los Condes and Sahagún was one of the most arduous and awe-inspiringly monotonous experiences I have ever had.

I walked across the flat meseta. Miles and miles of wheat and cornfields surrounded me. If I had collapsed in the waist-high wheat and corn, no one would have known except perhaps another pilgrim, who might have tripped over me yet never noticed that the bump in his path was a person.

The invisible and unpredictable stones forced me to remember the sports psychology of the Olympic athletes. Above all, remain relaxed yet alert. It required all the Oriental disciplines I had ever heard of. My new shepherd's staff was friendly, but I couldn't lean on it too much or I'd get slashed in the face by waving grain. My shoulders reminded me that my posture was slipping in my old age—and my feet? They were feet that could have belonged to Frankenstein, thick with calluses, like hooves.

I pressed on as though in a dream. Where was John the Scot? Where was Ariel? Where was the Polo Lounge at the Beverly Hills Hotel?! On and on and on for ten hours that day, I trudged, slowly recognizing that if I didn't understand and *accept* what was inside of me as a human being, I couldn't understand anything else in the world . . . not really. I . . . we . . . as individuals, were the problem. The world would become a happier place when each of us understood who we were. How many times did I have to realize that?

✳　　✳　　✳

My friend Anna had had a relationship with a man who lived at the edge of the meseta. She said he lived in a place with a red roof and a restaurant and bar. She said he would greet me with open arms and give me orange sodas and Popsicles.

His name was César, and he had been her love affair on the Camino. He lived with his brother and tended to the pilgrims who made it across the meseta.

She had collapsed in the wheat fields on her journey and had had an experience of realization unlike any other. She said she thought she was going to die when she fell. She couldn't go on and had run out of water. She saw a light that she interpreted as God. A voice then told her to get up and continue. She said she felt a love from that light that was so inspiring she couldn't describe it.

I thought of the time my father had cracked up his car. He said he had been unhappy and had had a few drinks. He said he felt himself leave his body and begin to travel very swiftly toward a bright white light. He said the light was so awe-inspiringly loving that he wanted to go toward it more than anything. He said it was pure love. Then, he said, he thought of the people who needed him. The moment he had that thought, he was back in his body, racked with pain. But he said, "I know I died that day, and it was so beautiful that I'm no longer afraid of death. It wasn't my time then, but when it is, I will see that light and that love again."

Anna described her experience in the same way. Of course I had heard of many people having a near-death experience that was nearly identical. They also spoke of seeing dead relatives and loved ones.

Was that what I was looking for? I didn't see any light, but I did have conversations with people who were no longer in the body. Perhaps because I already knew about the light and the continuation of the soul, I was able to accept their lessons in my head. I had heard Olaf Palme and John the Scot speaking to me. They were real. They were not physical, but they really existed. Where were they now?

After ten hours of the meseta, just as I felt near to collapse, I saw the red roof. And there was César with outstretched arms, just as Anna had said. The people who lived along the Camino somehow knew the progress of the pilgrims they were interested in. Anna had called him and asked that he look for me. Others ahead of me must have informed him.

And there he was. I staggered toward him. He handed me an orange soda and led me inside. He was about thirty-five, tall, dark, and very handsome. Anna had good taste.

The restaurant-bar was modern, neat, clean, and inviting. "Come inside," he said to me in perfect English. "Whatever you want is yours. And if you want me to send anything home for you, I will." I wondered if I could send part of myself home.

César's brother came from rooms upstairs. Other pilgrims slouched in the chairs next to tables. Nobody could speak from exhaustion. The brother brought me salad and bread. He knew I couldn't eat more than that.

"You are well on your way to finishing the Camino," said César. "Have courage. Don't stop now!" I couldn't have stopped if I'd wanted to. How would I get to an airplane?

The brother asked if I would like to nap upstairs. I declined, knowing it would break my rhythm.

They sat with me. I looked closely at César. Anna had known him for three days and said the love affair had contributed greatly to her marriage because it had given her variety and she felt she had fulfilled the requirement of falling in love along the romantic, feminine path. She was more happy with herself because of César.

He asked about Anna. I told him how fond I was of her and how she had helped me with this incredible experience. He nodded, saying she had been helpful to him too. I didn't ask how.

I spent a few hours talking and resting with them and some other pilgrims. They were so kind and accommodating and would take no payment from me.

Here were two good-looking brothers living in the middle of an empty, unforgiving plain, serving the pilgrims in any way they could.

Maybe they weren't so isolated at that. I'm sure many a female pilgrim looking for the meaning of life found the answer for a day or two with them. I knew I'd never see them again, and I was impressed—not enough to get me upstairs . . . but impressed.

I said good-bye to their oasis near Calzadilla de la Cueza, thinking that sex was like the Camino, a dance between what one wanted and what one needed.

13

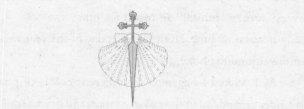

Some hours later the crippled man in the wheelchair whizzed by me in some sort of cosmic travel trance of his own. Whenever he arrived at *refugios*, people generally accommodated him because he seemed to operate with an unswerving sense of divine trust. He never had any money and was incapable of taking care of himself. It didn't matter. God was his copilot.

On the way to Sahagún a man on a bicycle stopped me. He had regards from Javier, who said he would meet me somewhere on the Camino. I blinked, remembering what John the Scot had told me.

He also said the singer from Brazil had very bloody feet and was two days behind me. He said her husband was two days ahead. I never even knew she had a husband. Maybe the husband didn't know it either.

It was customary for pilgrims to leave each other messages in the *refugio*'s guest book. I had a message from the Irish girls. "Be careful of Javier. He is a sex maniac and tries to crawl into every woman's bunk!!" So much for him.

It was now June 21, the longest day of the year and the day of the summer solstice.

As I walked I began to see different colors of purple and lavender embedded in the colors of trees and grass. I squinted my eyes and opened them wide again. I couldn't compute the colors I was seeing. Then I remembered that the spiritual masters said that you begin to see the divine shades of lavender and violet (the colors of the crown chakra) when you become attuned to the fourth dimension of reality. The third dimension was the physical dimension of reality as we know it. The fourth is the dimension of perception beyond the physical. They said that violet and lavender become more discernible when a human being realizes that the spiritual dimension resides in everything that is alive. The spiritual dimension, they said, was the true reality. They went on to instruct that we had been programmed to create problems for ourselves—psychological, physical, and even spiritual problems. Therefore, we were not prepared for peace. We didn't even really desire it because it wasn't a familiar emotion. In fact, they said, most people would find bliss and peace boring.

But we didn't need to learn about awareness through pain and turmoil and conflict anymore. It was time for a new understanding that our fundamental identities were spiritual and peacefully balanced. We had just lost sight of that. Again, they said we were essentially spiritual beings living in the physical. Our identities were correctly defined as soul beings, not physical beings. We somehow had it the other way around. I wondered how that had happened. In a few days I would find out.

When I reached Sahagún, I called Kathleen again. She said she had mustered the energy and had gone to Paris one last time. She knew she would never see it again. She said she saw new colors in the flowers, the people, the markets, and even the air.

"Everything seems so beautiful to me now. Why didn't I see this beauty before I knew I was going to die?"

"But you're not going to die," I said. "You're just going to pass on."

"To what?" she asked.

"To your next experience, I guess," I said. "And I think you'll find it beautiful there too. You're already seeing glimpses of another dimension, aren't you?"

She hesitated. "Yes, I am. Is this what you've been talking about all these years?"

"Yep."

"Did you tell me your father had seen incredible beauty when he was dying?"

"Yes," I said. "And he used to tell me about seeing his long gone relatives during his dream state. He said he knew they'd be there waiting for him."

There was a long silence.

"Oh, God," said Kathleen. "When I see Ken again, will he drag me down to the bottom again?"

"I don't see how there would be a bottom in heaven. When you're there, you're there."

"Do you think we lost paradise on earth?" she asked.

"Yes. But I don't know how it happened."

"Will you know by the end of your pilgrimage?"

I didn't know what to say. I decided to tell her some of my experiences with Ariel and with John the Scot talking to me and what I was learning. Then I told her that I hesitated to tell anyone else because they would think I was making it up or I was crazy. They would also think I was a colossal masochist.

At the end of my explaining all this, which I thought would be very disturbing to her, she said, "When you decide to tell anyone else, do it on your terms. It is your truth. Everyone has his own reality anyway. My reality has always been so intellectual. It takes my dying to find there is another one."

She talked on for a while longer. Then she said, "Don't worry, I'll be here when you get back. I want to hear more, and I'm sure there will be more."

We hung up.

Soon after that a man walked up to me. He was with his dog and said he had been walking for seven years!

In every village I was awed by the opulent richness of the churches, while the poor people who attended them gave every last penny they had to the collection plate. One priest sold holy candles to the peasants, which they lit, placed on the altar, and prayed over. When they left, the priest put them up for sale again. They had paid for the privilege of praying.

I sank to my knees in a grove of trees and lay down. I had left a pair of panties and socks drying on a windowsill somewhere. I thought about how I missed them and how necessary they were. I punctured a blister on my right heel and sewed the skin together so it wouldn't rub. I put my hat over my face and fell asleep, hearing the trees sway over me. Then I saw flashbulbs in my head and heard someone asking me questions. I opened my eyes and saw a band of journalists over me. Then two paramilitary men got off of a motorcycle, walked toward me, and shoved their cameras in my face. I made a decision. I simply turned over and went back to sleep. When I woke up, everyone was gone. Passive resistance worked.

I continued on to El Burgo Raneros. The village looked like something out of an old John Ford movie. It was "Western" with windswept adobe buildings like those in Arizona and New Mexico. It even had a Western-style bar that made me think any minute I would see John Wayne come striding through the door. I found a machine with orange sodas and entered the bar.

A woman came over to me and offered to wash my clothes. She invited me to her quarters above the bar, where I sat in front of a TV set and watched a bullfight. I browsed *El Pronto* magazine as she fixed me *minestra* with potatoes and onions.

She offered to take my backpack to the next town, Mansilla de las Mulas, the next day. Yes, it would be a miracle to walk without weight.

I thanked her and retired to the *refugio* across the windswept Western street.

The next morning there were members of the press sitting in the *refugio*. They were interviewing the other pilgrims about me.

I dressed inside my sleeping bag and left by the back room with my backpack, which seemed heavier than ever. I couldn't wait for the lady of the bar to take it for me.

I was moving in a surrealistic dream now, through some of the most ancient and beautiful cities in Spain. I had lost Carlos and Ali. The Germans, when I saw them, were always drunk; the Belgian man who was my brother in another life moved ahead with his baseball bat, determined to beat all records, and the Irish girls were long gone.

León was the most impressive of the ancient capitals of Christian Spain in the tenth and eleventh centuries. It had been invaded and conquered by the Moors in the eighth century, and its medieval history was one of continuing battles between Christians and Moors. The city was essentially a fort ringed by walls as it stood surrounded by plains. It was the city of kings. I felt I had been there. At the Hostal de San Marcos, a refuge and monastery dating from the Middle Ages, the monks gave me a ration of food—bread and cheese and wine. I sat in the church trying to tap into the familiarity I was feeling. I stood up and, as though guided, began to explore the ancient streets of the old city. I looked in shop windows as though I was searching for something.

Then I saw it. There was a jewelry store that sold antique artifacts. Slowly I walked toward the display window. There, at the side of the display, was a small golden cross. I went inside and inquired about it.

"It is Moorish," said the salesman. "It has been handed down through the centuries. Interesting and quite rare, because it could be Christian as well as Moorish. It could also have been designed from the ancient Egyptian symbol for good luck."

"Do you know who it belonged to?" I asked.

"Oh, no," he said. "Probably many people. Legends spring up about these ancient pieces. But we do know it came from the time of Charlemagne. I've never seen one like this one."

Tears sprang to my eyes. I was back on the Camino in ancient days. John the Scot placed it around my neck as I came out of the water he had pushed me into. I remembered fingering its thin gold and wondering why it meant so much to Christians. I remembered that the Giant Moor had given it to

John to give to me. Now, twelve hundred years later, had I found it again?

"Could I buy it, please?"

"Certainly," he said. "Would you like a gold chain to drape it on?"

"No, thank you," I said. "I'll just put it in my money belt."

I don't remember what it cost. I paid with a credit card.

Was it the very same cross? Or could it be one just like it? No, I didn't feel that. I felt I was holding the very cross that John the Scot had baptized me with, the very same cross that still reminds me each time I look at it of this experience through time and space.

I walked through the streets of León in a state of truth-shock. How would anyone believe this? Then I thought, So what? I had seen what I had seen, and now I was holding a third-dimensional, earth-plane proof of something I had experienced one thousand two hundred years ago. I held the cross in my hand and walked on.

* * *

The Camino outside of León crossed a bridge over the river Bernesga. I passed scrap heaps and rubbish dumps and warehouses. I walked faster. I crossed streams, where I dunked my head into the cold water. I chanted "I am cool and I am peaceful" to myself in rhythm to my steps. I saw pilgrims pass me in taxicabs and buses. Anna had said I would be able to walk forty-five kilometers (about twenty-eight miles) a day by the end. I saw one Spanish girl walking with no shoes. I saw some prisoners doing the pilgrimage who would be released on good behavior if they completed it. I stopped at every stream and took the time to soak my bare feet in the cold water before I Vaselined them again. I sat gazing at the cross. I wanted to talk to John the Scot, but he had deserted me. I was lonely for him.

I passed the Roman ruins and Christian cathedrals of Astorga. I was now an awe-inspired tourist of my own past as I attempted to remember the places while not taking too much time.

On through the cities and villages I walked, with my cross as my protector.

My nights consisted of sleeping on floors in my sleeping bag or dream-walking through a new friendship with people who felt exactly as I did. We all felt we had been here before. We wondered whom we had been to each other. Then we separated and moved on, wondering if we were ever to have some fateful appointment with each other, each pilgrim buried in his or her own prison of stamina, exhaustion, confusion, and pain, longing for the revelation and enlightenment that would make it all worth it. We spoke of the Knights Templar in the ancient days and their fierce protection of the pilgrims, who were simply searching for the God within themselves and did not deserve to be robbed and terrified by bandits. We were grateful that the Spanish government protected pilgrims.

I told no one about my cross. I might have known these pilgrim-strangers in the past, but I didn't know them now. I would protect my cross at all costs. Was this being a Christian missionary?

Everywhere I walked there were monuments to Saint James—Santiago—the patron saint who was said to have protected the Christians from the Moors. Which one was I now?

I passed the Hospital de San Francisco where it was claimed that Saint Francis of Assisi had convalesced on his pilgrimage. So he had had physical problems too?

Roman thoroughfares led in and out of cities and to the moorlands on all sides, and as I walked the countryside and through villages and towns, some of the pictures in my dream-visions flashed before me again. I knew these places; I knew the terrain and the Camino before it had been built up through the ages.

Many churches along the pilgrim's way had been built by the Knights Templar. One in Rabanel was dedicated to Santa María and included the remains of its original twelfth-century Romanesque structure. Here in Rabanel, medieval legend has it, one of Charlemagne's knights married the daughter of the Moorish sultan. I saw the wedding in my mind's eye. I knew her, but I didn't know why. Charlemagne and his army took the pilgrimage on orders "from above." I saw him again with me by his side discussing God and the stars and what the Christian pope desired for him to do in the name of Christianity. I remembered that the Camino amplified all human emotions and confusions in an attempt at clarification. The conflict among humans was always about the interpretation of God. What was God? What did he desire for us? To whom did he authentically speak? Were Moslems heathens and were Christians infidels?

Then before I realized it, I was in the *refugio* outside of Foncebadón, the abandoned village of the wild dogs. And the Camino went straight through it.

I knew none of the pilgrims in the *refugio*. It was as though a new set of players had entered my drama. I realized the necessity of friends.

I sat by myself, feeling more alone than I had since Anna had left me in Pamplona. I had come more than halfway across Northern Spain; had realizations that major psychics would marvel at; survived hills, streams, deserts, and the press; and now I found myself afraid of a pack of dogs. I tried to calm myself. I was afraid of the pack mentality. It was terrifying to me. I remembered the huge black dog Anna had prayed in front of. I remembered hearing about bloody encounters others had faced. Had they just been being dramatic for storytelling purposes?

The strange pilgrims around me seemed oblivious of the danger in the village ahead of them. Perhaps they didn't know. Perhaps it was better to be uninformed—an ignorance-is-bliss sort of thing.

I turned my cross over in my hand. Then I heard familiar voices outside.

I ran to the entrance. Carlos and Ali stepped off a bus. So did one drunk German walker. I hugged them all.

My friends had come to walk with me through fear.

Ali and Carlos seemed like an old married couple. The German had a bottle of beer he chugalugged.

We talked of how we thought we wouldn't see each other again, and yet here we were. Was this our appointment in Samarra? Was Foncebadón going to be our bridge of San Luis Rey? I said nothing like that to them.

But I did bring up the dogs in the village ahead. All three dismissed the danger.

Oh? Okay.

Ali sat down, creamed her face, and put her hair in curlers. Carlos attended to his camera, and the German drank beer.

Was I the only person here who felt fear?

I tossed and turned in my sleeping bag (which wasn't easy), and when I woke, I felt a kind of protective presence. It was accompanied by the smell of vanilla. I looked around to see if someone was applying perfume. No. This was not the place. People were dressing and sleepily muttering among themselves.

The sweet vanilla scent grew stronger. It was Ariel!

I took some yogurt from my backpack and ate it. Ali combed out her curls. She looked quite lovely. Carlos tossed her a few good-natured jokes about her spoiled vanity. She coyly waved him away.

And I, observing this reality surrounding me, felt myself somehow outside of it. Ariel was still with me.

We began the trek at seven A.M. The others in the *refugio* were gone. It was good to see Carlos and his purple knapsack and Bermuda shorts and red socks. And Ali was using a staff to help herself. A new acquisition, I thought. I wondered if she had made friends with her staff. We walked for a few hours, talking quietly among ourselves. Then a sort of sixth sense overtook us.

We saw the village of Foncebadón looming eerily in the morning mist, mocking every Hollywood special effect I had ever been a party to. I felt a pang of fear as I clutched my cross. Then Ariel said, "Stay calm. Don't attract chaos." I relaxed a little. I turned on my tape recorder and then was afraid to talk into it. I walked silently. So did the others. We reached the crest of a hill and looked down. There it was. A curl of smoke rose from a hut. An old witch was supposed to live there, surrounded by no one but dogs.

We approached the village step by step, and suddenly we were in it. It was completely silent. Broken-down abandoned buildings and the remains of demolished structures stood like beacons from the past in the morning light. What had happened here? I heard cowbells in the distance and had to maneuver my way through cow droppings on the cracked cobblestoned streets.

I looked around at our group. Carlos and Ali had separated. Carlos was up ahead with the German man, who had not yet had a drink.

I was in the middle, and Ali brought up the rear. Then I heard a dog bark. It sounded small and insignificant, like a harmless dog on a neighborhood street. My heart began to pound. "Calm," said Ariel. I kept walking, clutching my staff in one hand and my cross in the other. I had almost canceled the pilgrimage because of this place, this moment in time. Then I remembered the Hopi remedy to calm dogs. I formed a beautiful red heart in my mind's eye. I filled it with as much love as I could summon and sent out my visualization. I felt the heart go out to dogs that I as yet couldn't see. Then another dog barked. I reinforced the heart to the dog I couldn't see. In fact, I saw nothing moving anywhere except for Carlos and the German and the smoke curling from a hovel up ahead. That was where the witch lived?

"Continue walking," said Ariel. I obeyed. Then I heard Ali sneeze. I turned around. Ali smiled. Carlos and the German were still in front of me, walking undisturbed. I could now see cows dotting the surrounding hillsides.

"Continue walking," Ariel repeated. "You fear nothing but fear. You create the fear. Fear itself does not exist. You know that. You know that."

Yes, I knew that. I walked, sending out the heart image, as alert as I had ever been. . . . Then I heard no dogs at all. And I realized I was through the abandoned village. This was it? This was what I was afraid of? Still sending out the heart image, I continued up the hillside.

Suddenly, I heard Ali scream. My heart froze. I turned around and looked at her. "My stick," she yelled. "I've lost my stick. And there are too many flies and insects."

Flies? Insects? Amazed, I realized that I hadn't been bothered by them. I never even saw any.

She called again. "I can't walk without my stick. I'm out of breath, and I can't walk." She was leaning up against an abandoned building, surrounded by cow dung.

"Keep walking, Ali," I shouted. "Step over the cow shit and just keep going."

"I can't," she yelled. "Someone help me. You know I can't abide this!"

Suddenly I felt disgusted with her. She yelled for Carlos. He turned around, saw her, and kept walking.

"German," she shouted, "come back here and help me." The German man obeyed.

I was then between some cows and Ali and Carlos. All at once, the dogs began barking again. They became louder. I was alarmed. What would happen now? I thought of moving on, but on the hillside I couldn't find the yellow arrow.

I shouted again to Ali. "Just move ahead, damnit," I yelled. She looked up at me on the hillside.

"Move!"

She slowly stepped over the cow dung. The German was on his way toward her.

"But I must have my stick," she shouted to him.

"Yes," he answered. "I will retrieve it. Where did you drop it?" He was running toward her.

"Back there somewhere," she said.

More dogs began to bark in chorus. The cows on the hillside started toward the village. Then I saw a pack of dogs skirt around the cows and head for the village.

Ali trudged toward Carlos. He yelled at her, "When will you learn how to think?"

The dogs were now a monstrous pack. I lost sight of the German. I sent out the largest love-imbued heart image I could muster.

Ali reached Carlos, and they had a shouting match as they began to run.

I couldn't spot the German. The dogs entered the village. I propelled another, stronger heart image. Then I saw the German. He was standing on a hill above the village with Ali's stick over his head, ready for combat. He was safe. The dogs turned and headed for Carlos and Ali, who were completely oblivious of the growing pack because they were arguing so intensely. My heart image followed the dogs. They suddenly became confused and looked up at the hillside toward me. Then they looked back at Ali and Carlos. Ali and Carlos had reached the main road above the town. They were safe and the German was safe. I scurried up the hillside to catch the main road.

En masse, the dogs turned and headed back into the village. I couldn't see whether they would test the fear of another pilgrim or whether they returned to herding the cows. I heard the ferocious barking fade in the distance as I walked on, wondering if someone else was having a lesson in his or her own fear. Out of breath, I stopped. I let the heart image go, and I thanked Ariel. But the angel was gone. I put my cross in my pocket. What I had feared most was over. And I had conquered the fear by being proactive with love imagery.

Ali and Carlos continued to argue. I encountered other vicious dogs on the trail after that, but I just kept walking, sending out the image. They barked and snarled their heads off, defending their territory, but now my territory was my path and I had claimed it.

I walked the Camino now with a calmness, and I walked faster because of it, sometimes doing forty-five kilometers per day, just as Anna had said.

14

After Foncebadón, Ali and Carlos and I separated again. I found myself able to do many things while walking. I ate food walking, arranged my backpack walking, drank my water walking, changed my tape recorder walking, fixed my camera walking, and took pictures walking. I found I was walking more on the balls of my feet because I felt lighter. The thistles cut my tights and my legs, but it didn't hurt. I got into a kind of spiritual march where the rhythm of my steps echoed my breathing. My shoes hit the dirt and my arms swung in rhythm with the thumping of my backpack. I swung my arms over my head so that my hands wouldn't cramp. When I stopped, I listened to the sounds of nature. Then I learned to *see* the sounds and *hear* the colors.

Was this freedom? No, it still wasn't. Real freedom would be to walk without shoes or a backpack or a staff or food or water, and mostly without thoughts.

The thoughts were what created the pain and anxiety and suffering. I remembered that the twentieth-century mystic J. Krishnamurti had said he was so pleased when he reached the point where he could walk in the wilderness without having one single thought in his head. He said he had surrendered totally to God. Like the ancient pilgrims, he walked in utter helplessness and knew he had found freedom. The saints saw angels as they walked and often produced miracles and proclaimed they were able to experience such things because of an abiding love of God. They talked of the awe-inspiring state of falling in love with God. I wondered if I surrendered totally to loving God, would I be afraid of *anything?* And would I even need to *think* anymore? The French writer Simone Weil once wrote of one's spiritual quest: "Only certainty will do. Anything less than certainty is unworthy of God." Should I then be "certain" of what I was seeing and experiencing on my own quest? Or should I doubt my visions? Was the conflict between belief and reality what we call imagination? If "reality" is defined by the truth of the five senses, then what was one to "think" of my experiences? Was there a difference between the brain and the soul?

The definition of "reality" changed with quantum physics. The great thinkers of quantum mechanics know that science and religion exist, however polarized, as methods of explaining the mystery of God.

Perhaps there were two realities. The material reality of the brain and the Divine reality of the soul. The Divine reality being the landscape of the soul, which knows and obeys no physical laws.

The reality of my soul seemed to want to communicate to me and to my brain and wanted to be understood and acknowledged and factored into my life today. In fact, my soul was entreating me to understand that *it* was the repository of all my experience down through time and that now as I walked, it was communicating such events to my brain.

I was feeling that my brain and my soul had merged and had become a medium for my understanding. My soul was knocking on the walls of my brain, longing to be acknowledged as the possessor of knowledge beyond my understanding. Was my brain beginning to open its doors?

✣   ✣   ✣

I felt I was somehow walking west to the edge of the world. And then I wondered: Was I walking toward the beginning of the world as we now know it? Would I finish the Camino where it all began? And what place would that be? The edge of the "known world," they said, was where the Camino finished—Finesterre.

What had finished? Was there a world before this that had somehow finished? Was the end of the Camino at the edge of the Atlantic Ocean in Spain called Finesterre because it was more than land's end? Had something gone before? Why had the legends said "known world"? What had been the unknown world? Then an idea struck me. Why was the ocean called the Atlantic?

When I realized that I was thinking beyond the "known world," I knew I had to do the rest of the Camino in another frame of consciousness.

I decided to say good-bye to Ali and Carlos for good. We had served each other, for whatever our reasons. I might be crazy, but there was now more for me than I had even imagined.

I talked to them about my feelings. They understood. We exchanged addresses and phone numbers. Carlos asked me for an autograph for his daughter. "I know we will never meet again. I have no interest in going to America. It's been very enjoyable knowing you, and I know we will never see each other again. Thank you."

I asked Ali if she would be able to walk alone. "No," she said. "I'm afraid. I'll take the bus alone now and then, but I'll continue to walk with Carlos when I can. I know you came to touch things within yourself. I came for a promenade. So you must now go on alone and do what you came for."

We embraced. I felt tears threaten, so I turned and walked away into the hills. As soon as I said good-bye, Ariel returned. The smell of vanilla was all around me. I began to talk to the angel. "Who are you?" I asked. "Have I known you from another time and place?"

There was no reply, only a stronger smell of the perfume as if that were the answer. I asked more. "Are you really an angel?" The smell increased. "Do we all have angels that guide us?" I asked. The smell grew sweeter and sweeter.

Then I felt the presence all around me. In front of me, behind me, by the sides of me, until I felt I was part of that presence. I began to laugh and giggle. I remembered how the current Dalai Lama would laugh and giggle for no apparent reason. It was a kind of secret laughter at the most unexpected moments, as though he was hearing something in his soul from the gods.

We had spent the better part of two weeks together in Brazil at the ECCO conference in 1992. Brazil—yes, many things had begun for me in Brazil. The Dalai Lama was such a jolly person, giving his lectures for hours on end with no notes, and always that secret, contagious laughter would permeate his wise words. And he was a flirt. A great spiritual master who flirted almost in a knowing way, though knowing sexuality wasn't part of the flirtation. It was a spiritual flirtation. I liked that—a flirtation of the spirit.

I skipped along a mountain path with Ariel beside me. Then I entered a small village with a stream and a kind of swimming hole. I stopped dead in my tracks. I felt another vibrational memory slide through me. Could it be? I recognized it. It was the stream where John the Scot had dunked me under and "baptized" me. I recognized the hills around it and the waterfall and all the terrain that must have endured down through the ages. I walked toward it. I felt the memory flood over me. But now there were young people splashing in and out of the water. I was in two dimensions. Some of the young people recognized me. Oh, God, I thought, I want to relive what went before. I wanted so much to have someone push me under the water in homage to John. I was so terribly hot. I hesitated, and then I made a decision. I released my backpack beside the stream in the same place I remembered having stood. The young people stopped laughing and stared at me. Would I or wouldn't I? In a new freedom and an old memory, I stripped down to my underpants and pushed myself into and under the water.

It was the same cold I remembered. The baptism rushed into my mind. I could feel John's presence. It felt like a tonic, a medicine of memory. The energy of John and the water rushed through me. The memories were part of me. I felt one with them. I stayed under the water, its pressure bringing everything back in the silence. Then when I felt that the past and the present had merged, I sputtered to the top, feeling I could spout Arabic as I breathed fresh air.

I looked around, expecting to see John standing over me, chanting a baptism, and Christian soldiers leering at me. Instead, I saw the young people. A crowd had gathered. Some of them applauded, others waved. I dunked and swam and dunked and swam. I became the cold and the wet and the sun above it. I laughed and giggled and sputtered. Then when I had had enough, I pulled myself out of the stream, wearing only underpants. The crowd applauded again. I looked around at them. There were no journalists. I dried myself and put my clothes back on. A few people ventured forward for my autograph, and I signed. One offered me a fresh bottle of water. I drank it and thanked him. I felt completely unself-conscious. It wouldn't have mattered to me if the press *had* been there. I had baptized myself into a new freedom and a new dimensional understanding. And I didn't care what anybody thought.

* * *

I walked on to Ponferrada, where the "real" world imposed itself again with its duality.

A press photographer in a white car stalked me and nearly ran me over. I didn't get upset. He enlisted the help of someone younger, probably his son, to harass me by yelling at me and throwing things. A picture of me angrily objecting would fetch a lot of money.

I began to play. I ducked and weaved across the street and slipped into a store. The store owner saw the commotion, recognized me, gave me an orange soda, and drove me to a place in the city where I could escape the vultures outside. He didn't know where the *refugio* was. It didn't matter to me which place or which city as long as it was toward the west.

He dropped me off in a nice hostel called Hostel San Miguel in Ponferrada. The woman proprietress gave me a small room, where I took a hot shower and washed my hair and underwear. My hands began to cramp. I couldn't finish washing. The cramps worked their way up my wrists and into my arms. I climbed out of the tub, grabbed a towel with my elbows, and headed for the bed. The cramps had spread to my shoulders and legs, which curled under me.

I was completely depleted of potassium.

As I lay there, I felt like a paralyzed mummy, looking like Ellen Burstyn in the transference of healing scene in *Resurrection*.

Soon I fell into a kind of reverie. Then it happened. John the Scot came to me again. He was smiling, his eyes twinkling in his ruddy, freckled face.

"Well, lassie," he began, "you baptized yourself into quite an experience, didn't you, eh?"

"Yes," I answered. "It was wonderful. But where have you been all these days?"

"Oh," he said, "I've been with you. However, it was better for you not to know it until you baptized yourself."

"Why?"

"You needed to experience yourself without me," he answered. "Besides, you had your angel, did you not?"

"Yes."

"God is the loving energy with which you create. Are you happy being suspicious of loving energy?"

"No, of course not."

"Do you not want joy?"

"Yes."

"Remember then that one drop of joy that you create transforms oceans of negativity. Suspicion of your dream is negativity. Be responsible for your dream. Your life is the dream you have created. I, whom you have created, am a tool to provide you with the knowledge that you already have. Have faith in the truth that you are possessed of all knowledge. In that truth, you know and are one with God. Your cross is the symbol of balance in all four directions. Whoever holds it anchors himself in the earth plane's physical dimension in order to know the joys and sorrows of life. The cross represents the resolution of earth-plane issues. That was the symbolism of the crucifixion. Jesus was the master of those resolutions and when he 'died' on the cross, he balanced everyone's issues alive on the earth at that time. He took the collective karma of mankind onto his shoulders during his crucifixion. That was why it was so painful for him. He initiated the consciousness of human life into the vibration of love. That is why it is said he died for mankind's sins. To be more accurate, he cleansed mankind's karma up to that point. Gave them a clean slate, so to speak. He was a true master, and he said, 'Ye will do as I have done and even greater.' He said the kingdom of heaven and God is within everyone."

"That is the God energy you're talking about?" I asked.

"Yes, it is felt as a love vibration. You experienced it in nature during your beloved musical storm, did you not?"

"Yes, and I have created you to tell me this because I already know it?"

"Most certainly," he answered.

"So I am having an internal dialogue with myself?"

"Precisely. Now trust that. It is really very simple. People will tell you, 'I wish I could believe that.' Well, if they wish it, they can. If you are truly aligned with the God vibration of love within yourself, you are always safe, peaceful and in surrender to your own true place."

He fell silent and I wondered if I was asleep and my "dream" was finished.

Then John said, "Now I propose that we continue with why you are doing this Camino."

"Yes," I answered. "Please."

"The Camino leads you west to the end of the known world, yes?"

"Yes. That's what the legends say."

"I will now show why you are walking toward the 'unknown world.'"

There was another moment of silence.

Then John said, "You must relax because I am going to

take you back to another time and place more magnificent than you can realize now."

I waited. I was suddenly nervous.

"You must let your consciousness go," he said. "Please remove your consciousness from standing in your way. Surrender."

I began to relax inside myself.

More time went by. Then, as though I was hearing his voice in another vibrational tone, my unconscious mind began to become activated and one with his voice. It is hard to describe what happened to me. In fact, I was not me. Not me as I knew me. In all the other visitations I felt I was me somehow. But that identity seemed to slip away from me now. . . .

15

Dear Reader, it is here, at this point, that I have debated with myself whether to include the ensuing events in the telling of my Camino tale.

I cannot deny that I experienced these events and occurrences, but I am also aware of how shocking and disturbing they will seem to those who have not contemplated such things. The Camino itself helps facilitate the resolution of emotional issues, but I was experiencing the deep and ancient spiritual reasons for the emotional confusions that conflict us in the first place.

What I will attempt to convey and describe may take you off the Camino path and to the edge of reason, but I have always felt that if one cannot walk to the edge of the precipice, then why walk at all?

There are many ways to experience one's spiritual education.

My heart began to expand as though the memory of what was about to occur resided there. I could feel a kind of soul-stirring heartbeat in my chest. My body seemed to be adjusting to something new inside me. I heard the echo of John's voice.

Then I saw a symbol like this:

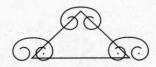

And John said, "The first injury to mankind was the physical separation from God and spirit, when soul entered mass. The first act of karma was fear."

I looked at the symbol, as he continued to explain.

"The triangle constitutes the trinity, which means the balance of mind, body, and spirit, or the God, the Goddess, and the Child. It represents the path back to God. Each spiral represents the balance of yin and yang, or male and female, in mind, body, and spirit. The energies fold in on themselves toward the center of the trinity, which is God. I will refer now to God as the Deity because that word is not gender based.

"In the first paradise on earth," John went on to tell me, "the first humans lived in a state of perfection. That is, each soul was both male and female. They devised a physical form in which to experience the simultaneous inclusion of male and female—the androgyne. The physical form perfectly reflected the soul—androgynous. Each human being lived in a state of androgyny.

"The time period was known as Lemuria. Mythologically, it was known as the Garden of Eden. Their spiritual state of being reflected a perfectly balanced physical form. Each individual's energy folded in on itself as the symbol indicates, facing the center of the trinity. The Lemurian civilization sustained itself for many eons. Then, as the soul forms became more adventurous to experience more outgoing physicality, a decision was made. They elected to separate the yin from the yang, the male from the female. They divided themselves. 'Out of the rib of Adam, Eve was born.' This story in your Bible is accurate," John told me, "except that it was symbolic of what came to be called sexual division. It marked the end of the Lemurian civilization and the beginning of the Atlantean civilization. This is the link," he said, "that you have been searching for. With the act of sexual division, which took eons of time, humankind found itself separated from its other half. In that realization fear was born; fear of isolation, loneliness, and more separation from the perfect soul balance, which reflected the Deity.

"Now you will experience what occurred, because you went through one of the earliest sexual divisions. Please do not be afraid. Remember you will only reexperience what you have already been through."

My heart began to expand more.

I was aware that I was receiving help in relaxing. Time passed. Then I began to see a fusion of colors through my heart, not my mind. The colors swam and undulated in and about the canals of my heart as though they were rivulets on a wide liquid heart canvas. At first the colors were predominantly green, blue, and violet. Then they began to take shape into solid objects, which took on deeper yellow, orange, and red tones. The colors slowly formed into moving objects until I understood in my mind that I was seeing a panoply of multicolored trees, flowers, and plant life. There were fruit-bearing trees bending in a gentle breeze ranged alongside well-manicured courtyards and multi-colored gardens. Fountains of blue-green water rose to the sky, and the sunlight was diffused by mist. Arched Oriental bridges over gurgling hot streams connected one courtyard to another. Adjacent to the courtyards were pyramidal structures, some of stone and others of crystal. Mosaics adorned the sides of the pyramids, and surrounding the mosaics were hieroglyphics.

As I became more and more aware of my surroundings, I also became aware that a gentle but full silence prevailed. I heard the sounds of small animals and the rustling and movement of the flora and fauna, but that was all. Yet I could "feel" them communicating with one another. I looked up and over at one of the multicolored courtyards. Coming toward me across a bridge was a tall, stately human being. His skin was golden-orange and his eyes the color of violet. He was very tall—nearly seven feet—and long blond hair hung from his head. There was no body hair on his face or arms. He wore what looked like a white Middle Eastern djellaba and sandals. He glided silently above the ground as he walked toward me.

As he came forward, he said nothing in a spoken language, but as a thought pattern he communicated, "Hello. I am John the Scot from an earlier incarnation." He smiled. I recognized the voice in my mind and also smiled. "Welcome to your original home," said John. "I will help you become reacquainted." I tried to answer, but there was no sound. Suddenly I became aware that John was communicating telepathically in a kind of visual-emotional language. "Simply think what you feel," said John, "and I will understand your communication."

I centered all my concentration on asking, "Is this how everyone here talks to each other?" I formed the words in my mind, but as I did it, I was aware more of the emotional intensity under my words than the specific words themselves. Then my feelings actually began to become visual in my mind. John smiled. "Yes. I understand," said he. "Good.

"Our greatest achievement," said John in my mind, "is the total unity of thought. We are not divided separately from one another. We understand, collectively, the individual's needs separately. We think of the welfare of each as though with one common mind. For we each perceive the other instantaneously."

We walked together. I realized I was feeling much lighter in body weight. I looked down and realized I was walking on a crystal path. "The crystal," said John, "is for thought amplification. We build many structures out of crystal because crystal amplifies thought waves, just in the same way crystal sets in your radios magnify sound waves. Crystal pathways also aid in meditation as we walk." As John communicated explanations in his telepathic way and as we moved together, other beings passed us on either side. They were dressed in either robes or loincloths and sandals like John, and were just as tall as he.

I gazed at the terrain around me. It was alive with color and life—multicolored flowers, fruit trees, prolific tropical plants, flora and fauna of every description—and all the plant life seemed to vibrate on the same wavelength as the human. I could feel the intertwining flow of energy, almost as though I understood how the animals and flowers were feeling and what the fruit-laden trees were thinking.

"We are mental gardeners," said John. "You know even in your present life that your plants have emotions. Human thought and activity affect them. So it is in Lemuria. We are in complete harmony with the molecular properties of plants and animals, and through mind projection we nourish them as we nourish each other."

As we walked, John reached into a tree and plucked a ripe rose-colored fruit. The air had a perfumed lilt through its branches. I could hear children's laughter like tinkling birdcalls in the distance. Then I heard a bird answer back. I looked up at the fruit tree and smiled. I was certain the branches bent toward me.

"This fruit is the mainstay of our diet," said John, as we both ate the juicy fruit. "It is what you know as the mango. The mango has perfectly balanced yin and yang properties. When digested properly, it stimulates the correct patterns for the projection of telepathy. Since our purpose on earth is the high development of mental harmony, we use the mango to help us."

I walked, thinking to myself. The perfumed fragrance in the air seemed to follow my thoughts as I moved, wafting and rolling with my own vibrations. I was beginning to feel caressed by the harmony of Lemuria. Lemuria *was* a veritable Garden of Eden. I suddenly understood the symbolic description of Eden in the Bible: total peace, total beauty, total harmony. I wondered about Adam and Eve and the temptation of the fruit from the Tree of Knowledge. What was the apple?

Just as I thought the thought, John answered me. "I will explain the fall of the Garden of Eden later, because you were a part of it. It would be better for you to reexperience it rather than relearn it through words, but that is some time away. You have much to see first."

As we walked, I saw other beings meditating in levitation three feet from the ground above the crystal paths. "Some of the beings are priests," John explained, "who wear crystal headpieces for even more intense thought amplification." In and around the lush gardens were pyramid structures carved in crystal or stone. Some of the pyramids were encrusted with gem-stones of emerald, ruby, sapphire, and jade. The gems had prop-erties reflecting the electromagnetic fields of the earth, since they were formed as a result of natural earth pressure. "They are extremely valuable," said John, "because they also heal and aid in thought amplification." Layers of bright green vines wound around the base of each crystal pyramid.

John led me through the misty, lush tropical gardens and talked into my mind. He explained that Lemuria had fifty mil-lion souls of predominant races (the races that we know today plus two more—the golden-orange skin with violet eyes, and the violet skin with violet eyes). The capital city was called Ramu, located where the Hawaiian Islands are now. Lemuria was divided into seven states, or counties, united under a sim-ple monotheistic religion and one system of thought. The tem-perature average was 72 degrees and was never lower than 52 degrees or higher than 102 degrees. It was essentially tropical, with no mountains but instead rolling hills and gently rolling plains. All the buildings were constructed to manifest the elec-tromagnetic frequencies of the earth's natural forces, thus giv-ing the humans higher forms of energy. They were, therefore, not an agricultural or horticultural society, but an ecological society. John told me that the life span of an individual in Lemuria was incalculable because the physical body, due to its harmonious properties, was immortal. However, after souls had reached a high level of seniority, they simply elected to dissolve the physical body to return to the astral plane. Their reason for existence was to manifest total harmony on a physical plane, and once that was accomplished, they could move on.

When John finished explaining, I began to understand more fully the basis on which the Lemurian lived. He was not technological in his superiority. He was a being who strove to be harmonious with all life around him. And the harmony was accomplished through unity. For all things affected one another. And the highest unity was with the Deity, for the Lemurian had come to realize that the most positive and dependable source of knowledge was the cosmic mind.

I followed John. I could feel myself communicate with the trees and flowers through the power of telepathy, and I could hear them respond. Even the animals along the way—small horses, dogs, cats, and the fabled unicorns, who had grown frontal horns as telepathic instruments—acknowledged my thoughts as we walked. Some responded by physical touching, others by standing on their hind legs. It felt very endearing to me. I remembered how I had loved such amenities when I was there. I touched the horn of a unicorn. It was made of smooth crystalized protein, which acted as a sensitive antenna. The unicorn brushed his face against my arm.

John led me into a Temple of Learning. It was of pyramidal shape and made of crystal.

"We can tune into the cosmic properties of our own minds with the help of pyramidal crystal," said John. "To us, the acquisition of knowledge is considered spiritual attunement. And the growth of knowledge is looked upon reverentially. That is why we constructed Temples of Learning. They are thought of as universities enshrined against time to preserve the accumulated knowledge of the Deity. We have what you would call religious ceremonies, which serve two purposes: one, we speak our silent adoration of the Deity, and two, we disseminate knowledge to each other."

I looked around at the other students. Some had short hair on top and long hair flowing down their backs, done in various shapes of braids and curls. Brilliantly colored feathers were used either as hair ornaments or as jewelry adorning their necks or waists.

John gestured for me to look into a meditational hall. Forming a circle, about fifty students were in deep meditation and levitating about three feet off the ground. The room had a blue, misty tint to it. There was no sound and no instructor. They seemed to be communicating collectively with one another. I could see their auras vibrating. I looked closely, and down the spinal column of each person I saw that their chakras were vibrating with light.

John smiled. "They have done their homework, so to speak," he said, and he laughed to himself. "But levitation is a primitive development of the dimensional abilities."

John turned me back into the open, airy hallway and then into a study room. There was no furniture as I knew it in the room. Instead there were platforms on different levels. And thin mats on which to meditate. White marble columns adorned the platforms. I felt peaceful as I looked around. John beckoned for me to sit cross-legged on one of the thin mats.

"Some of what you will reexperience," said John, "will be unpleasant. But you are here because you have matured enough to reexperience your own truth. Do you understand?"

I nodded.

"When we meditate," said John, "we prefer to do it collectively because we each derive more electromagnetic energy from the group. I cannot stress enough that we are highly evolved spiritually because we communicate TOGETHER and on all levels. We don't divide our thinking into separate thoughts. We are as of one mind. We strive for total harmony of all individuals. And harmony is LOVE, and harmony begets peace."

I sat relaxed. I reflected on my life in the twentieth century. So little of it was devoted to collective harmony. In fact, it seemed to be deliberately focused on individual separatism, individual competition, individual privacy, individual needs and desires, and individual happiness. With my modern-day mind, I barely understood the principle of collective harmony. It was not even attractive to me or the society I lived in. Twentieth-century Western society really didn't take spirituality seriously, either. The human soul itself was not even really recognized as a fact. And certainly in the Western world the idea of the pre-existence of the soul was basically considered heresy. The soul was spiritually brutalized every day in the course of our modern human life. As far as most Western people were concerned, the soul didn't exist. When one referred to population in modern times, it was fifty million people. Here in Lemuria, it was fifty million *souls*. Very little in modern times was designed for the peaceful nourishment of the soul. I thought that even our music brutalized the spirit of harmony. It was loud, discordant, and many times actually disturbing. Perhaps that was why so many people were turning to drugs, out of a desire for ultra-dimensional experience, which they sensed was part of their spiritual truth and knowledge. Music was only sound vibrations, so why couldn't it be used to heal or soothe? Why couldn't it be used as group therapy for harmony instead of discord?

My mind began to drift in free association. Simultaneously with my thoughts on music, I heard the sound of a stringed instrument strumming soft chords. John spoke in my mind.

"We use musical chords for healing," he said. "Everything in life is a question of electromagnetic frequencies. Musical chord vibrations and frequencies carry their own healing properties . . . a kind of sound therapy. Music plays an important role in a society—both positive and negative. You have already seen some of the negative results of discordant music in your modern world with drugs, crowd disorder, and violence. Harmony in everything is the desired effect because it is positive. Disharmony produces its corresponding malaise. It is not peaceful.

Modern people here have forgotten their ancient past, yet they long to reproduce it."

I sat listening to the harplike instrument. Its music was soothing and seemed to come, gently, from a distance. I felt John speaking to me further.

"Everyone here," said John, "depends on everyone else. If one individual lags behind, the entire community brings itself down to that individual's level so as to support his growth. The group is so focused on that individual's need that they literally develop almost an amnesia of other information so as to attend to the needs of the one in trouble. The community becomes a single mind until the needy individual understands. Everyone is his brother's keeper. Everyone is responsible for everyone else. No one is allowed to need or want. There is an ongoing dynamic of common leveling, because it is a joy to progress spiritually. Progress is not a burden here. Since we have no ego structures, we are ultimately optimistic in our power of positive thinking."

I suddenly felt very hungry. There was so much I didn't understand, and yet everything I was feeling felt familiar. I looked up at John, whose eyes were closed. I felt John receive the hunger thought. Still in meditation, John held his hand in midair, and by concentrating on the molecular properties of a mango, he materialized one in front of my eyes. He handed the mango to me. "Through spiritual understanding, no one is left wanting," said John.

I remembered how Jesus had multiplied the fishes and

loaves for the masses. I remembered how manna had appeared from the heavens for the Israelites who were starving in the desert. I bit into the juicy mango and thought that spiritual knowledge must be the same as scientific knowledge. I wondered what Einstein would have thought of this sojourn back into time.

John went deeper into meditation. I felt myself relax more deeply also.

"Meditation," said John, "is the best technique for educating."

I felt my consciousness go into a state of sharp awareness. I was deeply relaxed and, because of it, open to outside stimuli, yet I was impatient to learn and filled with an overpowering urge to try to understand the big questions. "How did life begin?" I asked. I could hardly contain the tumble of questions building in my mind: "What does it mean?" "What is life?" "What is a soul?" "Who am I?" Questions that I knew must have answers.

I felt John patiently stop me. "I understand your impatience," said John. "Yes, I will try to help you understand. But it is necessary for you to relearn what you have actually experienced."

"What I have experienced?" I asked.

"Yes," said John. "I will endeavor to help you grasp it more specifically."

I felt myself breathe more deeply, careful to allow all the carbon dioxide out of my system as I exhaled. I fell into a deeper meditation with only John's voice as an accompaniment.

"For you to understand more deeply," said John, "it is necessary to make another sojourn even further back into time. We must go back *beyond* time and space, backward before space and time existed, before there was movement. Back to nothingness, when there was, in the vast loneliness and nothingness, only one spirit—that which is known as the Deity.

"In the beginning, there was one consciousness, one Spirit, one Force, a single oneness. Encompassed in that oneness was the energy that would bind later together all things, all life, all thought, all deeds, all all . . . and make *all one*.

"Out of loneliness, the One Spirit began to move within itself. This One Spirit set in motion great wonders and creations. A pantheon of hydrogen gases swirled in and around each other until they became suns. Lightness and darkness and gaseous substances combined with nuclear activity created luminosity until the light became color. Ultimate mass and ultimate Spirit interacted as the cosmos was born, creating universes within universes, worlds within worlds, dimensions within dimensions. Yet still there was only one Spirit, one energy, one law, which set all things in motion, bound all systems together, making them total and whole within themselves. And all creation was harmonious, like symphonies creating a music of the spheres.

"Trillions of galaxies swirled and flamed in and around and apart from each other. While suns exploded and died, and others were created. The Cosmic Void of nothingness became active.

The Great Thought had acted. The Deity moved during seven great periods, and after the seventh period, the Deity rested.

"And now the raw universe was stable and harmonious. There was total harmony, total peace. But there was an incompleteness. There was quiescence within the Great Spirit, an aloneness in its Oneness . . . a stillness . . . a deep need. The Deity felt the need to experience the feeling of itself within self. It felt the need to become un-empty. It felt the need to FEEL. It felt that its creations meant little or nothing without feeling within itself. The Deity loved its creations and saw that they were good, but so as not to be alone in its oneness, it turned within and said, 'Behold, I will make the greatest creation of all. I will make life, and the life will be in my own image.' And so individual souls in the state of divine perfection and essence were born. Trillions of souls in the Deity's divine image, a pure white light, spread throughout the universe, then broke and formed into pairs. The soul pairs extended toward one another, all able to weave and interweave in and among each other without losing their sense of pairing.

"The Great Spirit created the pairs to be soul mates. Each individual of the pair was created both male and female, and therefore complete within itself. Each individual soul was of the combined genders, therefore neither dominated or was unequal to the other. The Great Spirit, aware of its own perfection, desired that its children be fulfilled within each other, that as mates of the soul they could bear witness to each other.

Thus, they were created in twos and were bound together from the beginning of time and would be bound together throughout eternity. Together they were as brilliant as a thousand suns, each of them a separate illuminating being . . . children of light . . . children of the Deity. And the soul mate children of the Deity were created with polarities within themselves, polarities of positive and negative, yin and yang, not unlike the natural forces that are at work throughout the universe, governing all activity. For without polarity—male/female, positive/negative, light/dark, up/down—there would be no action, no forces set in motion, thus no creation. For it is with polarity that there is creation—life . . . whether it is spiritual, scientific, philosophic, mathematical, or material. So the soul children of light were created to be companions to each other while at the same time serving as companions to the Deity, who was their creator and the Great Spirit that binds together all things.

"Over billions of years," John explained, "these souls evolved, charged by the Deity with being cocreators of physical life—trillions of pairs of soul beings tumbling and whirling and circling through space until some came to the planet earth itself, while others spun off to other planets in the galaxy to discharge their duties on other worlds. Some remained in the divine state, serving only the will of the Great Spirit, among them the souls called Michael, Ariel, Raphael, Gabriel. Among themselves they communicated as highly developed vibrations of light and illumination. They were mature and full and divine in their will, serving only the Great Spirit that created them, transparent beings of pure light. They had electromagnetic wings and spinal columns of seven bright lights in a vertical line, which were known as chakras or the organs of the soul. The archangels watched over the souls who were commissioned to earth. They watched the soul beings, each uniquely created for each other with their own light hues, color spectrum, and electrical oscillations, move in unbroken circles, just as the planets moved, the yin and yang being the polarity for their cyclical movement. The yin was the female aspect of each soul and the yang the male. The yin was the attractive energy polarity and the yang the active energy polarity. Both were equal, for without either, there would be no activity—no life. So with each soul, the full circle was complete, because each soul was androgynous.

"And each pair of androgynous soul mates had its own unique electromagnetic frequency in which they were both bound up.

"Their purpose was to bear witness to the Deity and serve the Divine will, which would in turn be serving their higher selves. And to do this, the Deity gave the children of light the greatest gift of all—free will: the ability to set oneself free, to choose one's own master.

"With the first wave of souls that came into the earth plane, a metamorphosis occurred. As their light shifted to the earth plane, their crystal images began to take on the magnetic frequencies of the earth. As they tumbled and glided to the earth plane into ancient swamps and jungles, they became fully mature angelic beings with electromagnetic wings that reflected the electromagnetic lines of the earth. They had been given charge over the earth planet in the solar system. They were to be cocreators of the life-forms on earth, thereby expressing their own individuality in the process. The Divine Light had begun the process of life cycle, and its soul children of light were here to individualize it physically. They were free to have dominion over all life-forms. They were here to create new species and to help with the evolution of the life they created.

"And so the souls of light began to create life. A day could become a thousand years. Time had no meaning to the soul children. They would concentrate collectively with all the electromagnetic frequencies of their beings, until the object of their physical creation responded with life of its own. A lizard would grow and expand. Perhaps it would develop wings according to their prescription. Then slowly, iridescent feathers would appear. Millenniums became eons. Its head would begin to turn upward until finally, in a conclusion of blazing fury, it would flap its feathered wings and the giant, plumed, multicolored lizard would take flight—a completed creation of the invisible soul children of the Deity. Though they weren't aware of time or space, perhaps ten thousand years had passed.

"Hundreds of thousands of creatures evolved in this fashion. Through the movement of time and space, through the evolutions of their earth-plane work, the souls assigned to earth began to become fascinated with the physical earth. They began to move too close to the physical plane. Because the Deity had deemed them to be cocreators with It and because they had Divine capacities, they materialized life-forms and the life-forms were of fascinating interest to them. And being curious, and being of free will, they became enamored of their own creations. They created with all the universal Divine energies at their disposal. Life became a diversified field of play. They created beings of only yin energy frequency; they created only yang energy frequencies; they created mixtures of yin and yang and positive and negative. They created a panoply of diversity. Then they became seduced by the beautiful creations of their own making, believing that in many ways they had created greater beauty than the Great Spirit. Thus, they became rebellious in nature, moving closer and closer to their physical works and further and further away from the Divine Deity, until eventually they became completely attracted to their physical creations and actually fell from grace into the physical plane. Felled by the very forces of creativity that they had set in motion, they became one with their creations, rather than remaining in the state of oneness with the Divine Deity. Some of the creatures the soul children created were beautiful and harmonious, reflecting their specific creators, and some were so ugly and bizarre (reflecting those who were moving too fast) that they had to be devolved. Some of the souls became drunk with their ability to materialize and would not slow down, and their creations reflected their disharmony and went out of control.

"The archangels, Michael, Ariel, Raphael, and Gabriel, watched in disappointment as the virtual ballet of distorted evolution unfolded. They watched their soul brethren, out of control, begin to incarnate into the beings they so needed to control. This was the original fall from grace. Their fall from grace was so complete that they became that which they created, forgetting their divinity, and for the first time experienced pain and fear on a physical level. They lost their consciousness of being children of light and fell totally into the material plane, experiencing not only pain but sensuality as well.

"This is also what became known as the Lucifer rebellion or the Luciferian influence. *Lucifer* means 'light bearer,' as these souls of the Divine Deity were, but when of their own free will, they fell from the grace of the Divine, they created their own moral battlefield within themselves. The concept of evil, then, was actually the act of straying from the Divine Deity of their own free will. The Luciferian influence did not come from one evil being, but rather it was a collective mistake made by the original souls who forgot that they were created to serve the Deity with divine love toward all things.

"This was the first display of violence. Violence against the Divine laws. The souls began to argue and squabble among themselves as they went about creating more and more bizarre and distorted beings that reflected themselves. They created huge and useless and nearly brainless creatures such as the dinosaur. The conflict for survival of the fittest began, setting off for the first time upon earth the law of cause and effect, or the law of karma, because all energy always returns to itself. The creatures seemed to have demonlike forces in their natures, but they were, in fact, struggling against themselves. In doing so, they forgot to recognize each other.

"Fighting and killing broke out with the newly incarnated souls trapped in the denser physicality of the animal forms, giving them great pain. The archangels watched with disappointment, but remained detached.

"This was the fruit of their labors. These were the fallen angels. The archangels were witnessing the results of free will when it went beyond the boundaries of the Divine will. But they didn't interfere. They knew that the Great Creator Deity loved them all. The fallen ones may have felt separated and cast off from the Divine Deity, but not for all time.

"There were other beings in other worlds, in other forms, in other crafts, in other technologies—other brethren who had progressed more along the Great Spirit's way. And there were others who were experiencing circumstances similar to those on earth, and even others who were experiencing worse. In each case, every individual soul's task was to remember its own Divine nature and return to it.

"The Great Deity and the archangels understood that a purge of the chaos the souls had created would be necessary. A stop had to be put to the ever-evolving insanity that was building its future on earth. The denser life-forms, who were by now panicked with fear and distortion, had to be swept away. The life force then was cut off from these beings, bringing their vintage to an end. Hence, the extinction of the huge animals known as dinosaurs. The so-called Ice Age was not the reason for their disappearance. It was the vehicle through which they disappeared because their life force was drawn away by the archangels, who needed to create a more perfect environment for their soul brethren to redeem themselves.

"There needed to be a vehicle for the redemption of their souls on the physical plane. And so from the dust they created a new creature that would evolve to humankind . . . the primate.

"And so the lower primates began to evolve into the form of pre-man. In restoring order, the archangels needed to create a perfect form in order for the souls to return to their divinity. But the form and the souls needed to *evolve* together. The lost souls were now in an unconscious state, unaware of their divine origin, and unaware of their power and capabilities. This state of being came to be termed hell in the present world. Hell was being cast into outer darkness. Hell was being cut off from the illumination of the Divine Deity. Hell was a form of spiritual amnesia. This state was the result of falling into the physical and material plane in the first place. They retained their intelligence to some extent, but not their spirituality, therefore they were out of flow with the Divine will.

"And so the lower primates became the original vehicle

for man's evolution and return to the Deity, the first step for redemption.

"Evolving simultaneously in other parts of the universe in neighboring galaxies were other beings. Some had developed higher spirituality, some higher technologies, some both. The extraterrestrials, as they came to be termed, developed great crafts that traversed the planets. They traveled in these great machines carrying with them their cultures, their concepts, and their own developed ideas. Seeking to carry out the work of the Great Creator Deity, they observed the situation on planet earth and endeavored to speed along the process of evolution. They possessed high knowledge of genetic engineering and its codes and understood how long the process of redemptive evolution would take if left completely up to the primates. Thus, the extraterrestrials began the contributive gift of speeding up the evolutionary pattern by using crystal technology, genetic engineering, and interbreeding with the primates, both physically and psychically. This process was actually the missing link in the evolutionary line on earth. As a result of physical and psychic influences, man suddenly appeared with no seeming intermediate connection to the primates that preceded him. As a result of the extraterrestrial contribution, the souls were shocked back to consciousness. The more aware they became, the more complete they became, and thus the more the divinity of the soul shaped the physical body into a form that reflected the newly awakened divine soul itself, the physical body that expressed the perfect balance of male and female, yin and yang, the positive and negative spark that was the essence of the Deity.

"The ADAMIC race was created, and over millions of years it developed and evolved. It established rudimentary communities, customs, laws, and beliefs until a basic civilization began to form. And with the help of a second wave of extraterrestrials, the cradle of man's first flourishing civilization was born. The civilization came to be called Lemuria, and it was what the Bible referred to as the Garden of Eden. Now the vehicle for returning to the Divine was the Lemurian human. The extraterrestrials had accelerated the evolutionary pattern of earth's people."

There was a pause in John's discourse. John had been speaking on the creation of souls inside my mind, so vividly that I actually felt I had experienced it myself. He spoke of events that were unknown in our history books. He spoke of our fall from grace, our feeling of incompleteness, the original sin. He spoke of the missing link in evolutionary terms and said the psychic and genetic input of extraterrestrials from deep space was responsible. My mind whirled. I felt a kind of haunting understanding.

As he spoke and I sat in the Lemurian Temple of Learning, I felt every cell and atom in my body come alive. I felt free and as though I had been liberated from anxiety. I felt myself let go completely. I wasn't sure what it was I was letting go of until I realized I was levitating about three feet above the thin mat on the floor. I felt John smile. I felt one with John. I felt one with the Deity. I felt one with myself. I felt free. Adages and sayings and passages ran through my mind. "Know thyself." "The truth shall make you free." "Love thy God with all thy heart and all thy mind and thy neighbor as thyself." They had only been words before. Now they had meaning. My mind began to freely associate.

I remembered how affected I had been when I read Ezekiel and other books in the Bible that seemed to be describing spacecrafts and beings from other worlds (or the kingdom of heaven). And now John had explained what it meant.

I sensed myself vibrating in the air, feeling a peacefulness as great as any I had ever experienced.

"So then, visitors from outer space have been surveying this planet for millions of years?" I asked John.

"Yes. It is not unusual. It happens on every planet, so you mustn't fixate on the superiority of the extraterrestrials. I will explain. There are many breeds of extraterrestrials, some more spiritual than others. And *all* soul creatures are creatures of the Great Deity, charged with the same tasks—returning their souls to the Divine in exchange for having had the gift of life. This applies to the extraterrestrials too, though some of them may be of a higher spirituality and a higher technology. For example, when they arrived in the second wave to provide input for the Lemurian civilization, they brought art, culture, mathematics, and a higher technology and spirituality, but they also insisted on being revered as gods—as superior beings. They defied the

Great Spirit's law of humility and equality. They falsely represented themselves as God, and the by-product of their behavior was false idol worship. The archangels in charge of this galaxy were not happy with the spiritual falsehoods of the extraterrestrials and ordered a spiritual hands-off policy, which came at the height of the Lemurian civilization. They realized that it was better for humankind to work through its spiritual identity on its own until it could reach a more pure state of divinity alone.

"We arrived at a critical moment in the Lemurian time period," said John. "Atlantis, located in what is now the Atlantic Ocean, was an advanced colony of Lemurians," he told me. "Its inhabitants preferred to be called Atlanteans and preferred also to develop their own more modern civilization and break away from Lemuria, the spiritual motherland, because the Atlanteans were being greatly influenced by the modern technology of the extraterrestrials who had set up cultural exchanges there."

The extraterrestrials were highly evolved technologically, and the Atlanteans were becoming seduced by that technology— by their great spacecrafts, by their advanced material sciences, by their genetic engineering, by their art, and by their culture; and by what they believed was their advanced progress in social engineering. The extraterrestrials themselves were subtly trying to warn the Atlanteans to be cautious in veering away from their own spiritual underpinnings and were observing their policy of noninterference. But the Atlanteans were slow to take heed. Soon they began to develop the process of separating their thought patterns, the result of worshipping technology and material values. The motherland, Lemuria, was concerned that the new technological ideas would begin to dissipate the spirituality of Atlanteans and cause division and debate between Lemuria and Atlantis. They knew these ideas would ultimately affect Lemuria, the home of human spirituality.

Some of the Atlanteans who were practicing the new values would return to Lemuria espousing their new ideas and giving attractive examples of the extraterrestrial technology and art and culture.

John described what he saw in Lemuria as a result of the new ideas transported from Atlantis. He said the Atlantean ideas caused a division in the collective consciousness, which eventually caused a radical confusion in Lemurian communication patterns until most individuals reached a state of imbalance and disturbance, losing their identification with the unity and their identification with the whole. They entered into a state of alienation and loneliness. Out of this state of alienation, John said, "each individual developed the ego—or those feelings that would be 'of self' or 'selfishness.'

"This," said John, "was what you know as original sin."

He said the continuation of such "self"-concerned values meant the further development of a sense of superiority. And out of those feelings of superiority, one group of people would seek to enslave another group. The enslavers would mentally control those who had not reached a high enough level of growth and synthesis into the society. They would, therefore, be relegated to positions of lesser importance in the society, which would then lead to the evolution of a ruling class. When this happened, the destruction of the harmony of the ALL became complete.

John said that because the collective consciousness was destroyed and because the collective consciousness had previously been directly tied to nature itself, a great disaster occurred. The earth was a living organism responding in direct ratio to the collective consciousness of humankind—it was not the other way around. The collective spiritual consciousness of mankind actually molded and orchestrated the ecological movements of nature. The spiritual energy of man was more powerful than nature. The Deity made souls to be cocreators in life, with dominion over all life-forms. The earth itself lived as organically as a plant or an animal. It was alive with feelings and responses and emotional behavior patterns—and when the souls became distorted, disharmonized, and disturbed, so did the earth itself.

"So," John said sadly, "I saw Lemuria sink beneath the waves. So did you. The distorted electromagnetic energy of mankind disturbed the natural balance and flow of harmonious nature. And nature reacted accordingly. It saddened me beyond description and rendered me helpless. I heard so many millions of souls crying out for help because they did not understand what they had done. Volcanic activities beneath the surface of Lemuria became activated along the edge of the continental structure, and I knew Lemuria would go under."

I listened with a kind of wistful remembering. I knew I had been there when it happened, and I deeply perceived that the sinking of Lemuria set off a personal karmic reaction in my own life that I would be working out down through time— until I understood.

What was it I needed to understand? Why was I back in Lemuria now?

"Yes," John said, "you were there with me. You were my student then. You were part of . . ."

Suddenly, I heard a loud knocking. John's voice receded in my mind. I didn't know what was happening. I couldn't hear him anymore . . . only an echo. The knocking grew louder.

Then, as though through a protective tunnel, I felt myself racing into the present until I was specifically aware that once again I was lying on the bed in Hostel San Miguel in Ponferrada, Spain.

Someone was knocking insistently on my door. I didn't know at first where I was. I was drenched in perspiration. The real and present world was a shock to me. My body was foreign and strange. The sounds of construction in the street hurt my ears.

I walked around the room, trying to adjust. I felt confined and alone and very confused.

What had just happened to me? Had I had the most colossal dream known to mankind? What did it mean? Was it real? *What on earth was real?* Had my soul been talking to me? Was I having a spiritual awakening? In the end, was I first and foremost my soul, as I was in the beginning? And was I becoming a more expanded "me" now?

Slowly, I went to the door to find the proprietress of the hostel standing there with a man she had found who spoke English. She said I might want to sit with him downstairs for dinner so that he could deflect the press, who were also downstairs.

I thanked them, said I'd be down later, and closed the door.

Above all else, I wanted to understand what I had just experienced. Was it a dream? Was it my imagination? What was real anymore? Was I making up a past that had dramatic content even the poet John Milton hadn't imagined? In fact, what was imagination? What was its source, its motivation, its antecedent? Did imagination begin at the moment of creativity, or was it based on previous experiences and some kind of forgotten knowledge that my soul was communicating to my mind? As I made notes, I thought of a quote from the Tao Te Ching that impressed me. "Those who know do not talk. Those who talk do not know." Should I speak of it to anyone? No, not yet, I thought. Maybe never.

I dressed, joined the English-speaking man, had a dinner I don't remember, tried to pay for it but couldn't, and plotted how to evade the press in the morning while trying to find a yellow arrow in the middle of a city, all the while endeavoring to analyze whether I was suffering from some kind of psychological dislocation. The environment I was surrounded by was not harmonious to soul evaluation! I had to get out of the city. I only had a few days to go.

Was the past I had seen a part of me now? I knew my future would have its own unpredictable drama, but my present was a jumble of confusion.

I slept in that state of confusion. John the Scot did not come again. I tossed and turned, not knowing what was a dream, a vision, or what was real. Yet somehow I knew I was the creator of all these thoughts and feelings. Yes, I thought, had I created Lemuria, the fall from grace, original sin, and my separation from the Divine? Was that the message? Did we each create everything that happens to us *and* what we *think* happened to us?

16

The next morning I tried to pay for my lodging, but the proprietress wouldn't take any money. She led me out the back door, away from the waiting press.

Two simple Spanish housekeepers led me to the yellow arrow, and soon I was across the city and out of town.

I was walking through an orchard when, like a jackknife through flesh, a monstrous black dog leapt out at me from inside a tin barn. He went for my throat. But he didn't reach me. He was on a long leash, which stopped him in midair. The surprise felt so lethal. I regained my composure and walked on. At least I hadn't created him to bite me.

In Cacabelos I stopped at a small store. The owner came out, offered me wine and food. I took a few cherries. He then offered to send on whatever I felt was too heavy. I gave him some clothes and my precious packages of film. I paid him and gave him a contribution to the town's church. I thanked him, thinking how sweet the country people were to pilgrims. . . . I never received the clothes or the film. But what film could possibly do justice to what I was seeing in my visions anyway?

I began my ascent into the mountains toward Villafranca del Bierzo. They say that if a pilgrim makes it to Villafranca, he is absolved of all his sins. I wondered if that included fifteen million years of lifetimes.

Half an hour later, I had diarrhea from the cherries. I stopped and pulled down my shorts and squatted. A tall, thin man appeared from the trees. He wanted an autograph. I tried to shoo him away, but he, oblivious of what I was doing, wanted to talk. I ignored him and continued on with my business. He finally had the good grace to leave me. Celebrities *are* privileged—to have no privacy.

The next *refugio* was an abandoned store with a plastic cover over it. The temperature inside was 104 degrees. The man who ran it refused to let me use the bathroom. I asked him if I could wash my clothes. He said no. I spotted a dryer and said I knew how to use it. He said no.

I walked to the next town. The Camino here followed a busy highway. A big truck nearly knocked me over.

I now couldn't sit still for longer than an hour. So I kept walking. Through mountain country with frothy streams and cascading waterfalls. I was lonely and moody and irritated. I didn't care if I was lost or not. I was lost in time anyway. I only wanted to understand what was happening to my reality. Was this why people over the ages made the pilgrimage? Had any of them experienced the same thing that was happening to me?

The waterfalls came straight out of the rocks as I climbed. I passed pilgrims who were exhausted and sleeping along the way. What were they dreaming?

Each time I thought I had reached the level peak of a mountain, it stretched higher. My God, it was like life. I slipped in splatters of dung. I wondered if it was from animals or people. I wondered what would happen to sewers if people ate only mangoes.

Looking back down the mountain, I saw no pilgrims following behind. Many had taken to riding buses and taxicabs. No wonder.

When I looked back at the distance I had walked, my stomach turned over. Should we never know what was behind us or ahead of us? Should we just leave it alone? I was not who I thought I was. I was learning who I was before I became me.

I passed more shoes and socks, and trousers.

At the top of the mountain was a village. I saw a water fountain. On my way toward it, two more dogs attacked me. I ignored them. My focus was on the water. The dogs left me.

I drank the sweet water and dunked my head under it.

I made it to Villafranca wondering if my sins from past lives would be pardoned.

The yellow arrows took me along the Calle del Agua, where the Church of San Francisco stood in tribute to Saint Francis of Assisi's journey to Compostela. I wondered if his soul was somewhere alive in the world.

It was said that one should drink the wine of Villafranca sparingly because it burned like a candle scorching your soul. I could drink all I wanted because my soul had already been scorched.

I walked in a confused and painful reverie. Could I ever tell my dream-visions to anyone without seeing his eyes roll? I was basically a very "down-to-earth person" whom people knew to be skeptical and analytical about most things—why was all of this coming to me? Could ley lines really induce such memories? Perhaps because I was so down-to-earth, I could hear the earth's history, her experience. Was I hearing and seeing the earth's experience so vividly that I seemed out of this world? It took an act of control not to roll my eyes at myself!

I walked until sundown, not caring whether I'd find a village *refugio*. I didn't care whether the press would ambush me again. I stopped at an isolated spot under some trees in a field and unrolled my sleeping bag. I lay inside looking up at the stars. I could see the Pleiades and Orion. I remembered the reference in the Bible to the sweet influence of the Pleiades and the bonds of Orion. Had the authors of the "Book of God" known of the extraterrestrial influence on mankind? I gazed and gazed until I felt I could see between the air particles. What were the living beings on other stars doing now, this very moment? Were they gazing at earth? Was I being influenced by them in some sort of telepathic way? I knew we couldn't be the only life in the billions and billions of galaxies above me. What part had they played in our march of time? Or was I creating them, just as science had said we created time?

And what were souls made of? The stuff of God, as the Bible said? What was man and what was woman? If each soul was both masculine and feminine, then why the separation? As soon as that thought struck me, I closed my eyes and John came again.

Dear Reader, many believe that sexual union is the closest one can come to experiencing the Divine. I believe that to be one of the paths, and because of what I experienced I understand why sexuality is the basis in our world today of so much confusion, desperation, and desire for completeness.

Forgive the depth of my decision to continue if you find it threatening. On the other hand, it may be threatening and shocking *because* it resonates with your intuitive truth.

In a rush of energy, I swirled back in time as though through a tunnel of light. Back further and further until I was once again in the Temple of Learning in Lemuria. I was sitting beside John on the same thin meditation mat. I heard the same music as I had previously, and we were in the middle of our conversation and his dissertation on Lemuria. He made no reference to the interruption or that another few days had passed. Our conversation seemed to exist as an event beyond time that was etched in its own reality. Even his words were the same as they were when we were interrupted by the loud knocking on my door in the hostel in Ponferrada.

"You," said John, "you were my student. You were part of our program for improvement. We needed you. We needed everyone who could help stop the disharmony in Atlantis and the effect it would have on the motherland, Lemuria. Come with me."

I obeyed John. We walked from the Temple of Learning into the street. Brightly colored feathered lizards scurried across the crystal walkway. Three citizens sat lotus-positioned along the roadway in deep meditative states, others levitated and floated alongside. An iridescent peacock spread its multicolored tail and produced three long turquoise feathers for a priest who desired new feathers for his breastplate. The priest bowed his thanks. The peacock strutted on. Children played and I could feel their laughter and hear their joy.

John guided me by the arm. "Come," he said, "we have work to do through experience."

He led me into a crystal pyramid building. People in various stages of dress mingled about. In their silent thoughts I felt an air of reverence.

"These are the places where life begins," said John. "This is our alpha—our beginning. This is our portal for life. These are our birth chambers."

I looked around. Blue illumination lit the entrance hall. At the end of the entrance was a birthing hall.

"Come," said John. "We will prepare."

The birthing hall had a deeper shade of blue illumination. "A healing color," said John. All around the spacious hall were huge tanks made of crystal and encased in marble blocks. The crystal tanks had been carved in the shape of a womb. Inside was a golden-colored liquid.

"In the tanks the new child is born," said John.

I could see beings emerging from tanks on the other side of the hall, nursing their children as they moved. Attendants came to see to their needs and carefully dry the mothers and children. Then they scanned the newborn infants with large crystals.

"They are looking for physical defects," said John, "which should, if found, be attended to immediately."

John led me directly to a particular tank. Inside, a being floated peacefully. The hair was cropped short; the outline of the pregnant stomach was firm and full. The legs looked strong, the buttocks solid, and the back erect and straight—a classical figure, as perfect as a Greek statue, but both masculine and feminine.

John turned me away from the tank.

"These are our beginnings," he said. "Your heritage. Birth

is one of the most sacred moments in Lemurian life—and you are to witness this birth. We know or recognize no shame; therefore, as part of our Lemurian custom, we will remove our garments."

As if by ritual and prescribed ceremony, John began to remove his clothes. I followed suit. Over his head John gracefully pulled off his white robes. At first I was casual, then I found myself open-eyed in astonishment. John slowly, with no self-consciousness, removed all his clothing. He had breasts—female breasts. I didn't understand. I looked down. My mouth dropped open. John had genitalia that were androgynous. I looked down at myself as I removed my own clothing. To my own astonishment, I was androgynous also, with genitalia that reflected that. I looked back up at John. I didn't know what to think. John smiled gently.

"You see," he said, "even as it was in the beginning that the soul knew neither male nor female, so was it in turn with the Lemurian race. All souls were and are androgynous, and in a pure state of the divine; therefore, they bend and shape the physical body accordingly."

Stunned, still openmouthed, I turned around and looked into the tank. The being giving birth turned to face me, revealing the stomach and breasts and androgynous genitalia. All the male and female parts were included.

"This being will now go into labor," said John. "This new mother will manifest a child."

I stared at the mother being. Except for contractions around the stomach, there was no evidence of labor pains. She/he was in a deep sleep—self-induced. Then I saw the stomach begin to develop more. Time seemed to accelerate, and the stomach expanded more and more fully as a peaceful labor increased, until finally, the being giving birth had an almost totally feminine countenance. The breasts were full. The expression on his/her blue-tinged face was serene. He/she floated in the golden liquid peacefully. The legs opened and the birth of a new child began through a cervix and vaginal cavity. The new being passed into its new physical world. The small baby was also androgynous, but in miniature form. The child floated in the golden liquid.

Midwives entered the crystal tank and severed the umbilical cord. Now I realized that everyone around me was androgynous. They caressed and attended the baby.

I watched the mother. She/he had stopped floating and sank to the bottom of the tank. An attendant raced to a broad shelf, retrieved a crystal from it, and brought it back to the tank. Lifting the crystal, he scanned the body of the androgynous mother through the tank looking for life auras. There were none. The androgynous mother had died. I began to scream and to sob. I tried to control myself and to understand what had gone so terribly wrong.

"Look carefully at the being's face," said John. I obeyed. I stared closely through the tank into the dead androgynous mother's face. Then, forward through eons and eons of time my memory raced. I tumbled forward into time. And then suddenly I understood. The face was that of the one who would become Charlemagne and then Olaf Palme.

I fell to my knees. "Why?" I pleaded with John. "Why did this soul have to die?"

John touched my head. "Child, this being was your twin soul," he said, "and had a karmic defect that needed to be worked through in the Divine state. This soul succumbed to its own passing willingly, which may seem unjust in the short term, but in the long term was necessary. It was necessary for you to witness this again, just as you experienced it then, so that you might understand."

I looked into the face again. I could feel the tears on my own face, taste them on my lips.

"You saw this soul on the Camino," said John. "And you loved him in your present lifetime. You have just begun to understand the karmic role you played and will play in each other's lives through time. And you will experience each other again—and more than once. Now you are beginning to understand. It is painful, but truth is necessary and less painful than lack of it."

I felt my mind clearing with the meaning of what John was saying.

"Was he my soul mate, then?" I asked, feeling like an adolescent.

"No," said John. "A twin soul. You have been through many times and places together."

Then the real question struck me. "Why did I know this man later?" I asked.

John looked at me deeply. "That is what you will understand next," he said.

"Are twin souls or soul mates always incarnate together as opposite sexes?"

"Oh, no," said John. "Many times twin souls and soul mates incarnate as the same sex. That is why so many homosexual relationships and same-sex heterosexual relationships have been so deep and so positive. You see how sexual identity becomes irrelevant in terms of spiritual meaning? The body is as irrelevant to love as it is to death. Spiritual context is all that is important."

"So we are all basically androgynous?"

"That is correct. We have forgotten that each body should reflect the soul, which possesses a perfect balance of both yin and yang, positive and negative, masculine and feminine. We have stereotyped a separation. You will see the reasons for that soon."

"And what is the difference between a soul mate and a twin soul?" I asked.

"The soul mate reflects the identical oscillations of frequency as its mate. The pair of soul mates was created at the beginning of time. They are meant to be together and continually search for a reunion."

I wasn't certain I wanted the answer to my next question. "Is my soul mate incarnate now in the world?"

"No," said John. "And that is the reason for your continual search. You are really looking for the other half of your spirit."

I listened. John waited.

"And twin souls?" I asked.

"They are souls who have been together many times and serve each other's journey back to the Divine, as you have just realized. Twin souls often wait for reunion, so that one or the other can serve others."

I rose from my knees, looking at the tank. I leaned my head back into the air and sighed deeply. I closed my eyes for a long time. Then, together with John, I dressed.

"Did I have a child in this Lemuria?" I asked.

"You manifested pregnancy, yes," he answered.

"And did I self-perpetuate the process alone? Did I simply will myself to become pregnant? Is that how it worked?"

"Yes," answered John. "Through meditative communion you determined whether another soul desired entry. You chose to be a portal for that soul, and you simply impregnated yourself with your own androgynous desire. Your polarities of yin and yang were perfectly balanced. The new soul would enter, or incarnate, in your body after about three and a half months, or with the first movement. You were then a portal for another soul. It was a great responsibility."

I brushed my hands through my hair and sighed again. "To

allow another soul the possibility to come into the physical world must have been the epitome of the Lemurian experience," I said.

"Yes," said John. "It was considered the ultimate. And the offspring was raised by two androgynous beings who chose to make a life together."

"And were those beings monogamous?" I asked.

"Well, there was no such thing as sexual consciousness in that time, but yes, through one-on-one relationships a higher spirituality could be reached. Spirituality was stunted by diffusing the intensity of commitment to one being. It usually didn't occur with those who had chosen a mate through whom they could experience a pathway to higher growth. Do you understand?"

Yes, I understood, I thought. But I couldn't understand why so many fundamentals had changed regarding human life now. John heard my confusion. "You will see very soon," he said. "That is why you are here. The human race needs to understand that it is meant to reflect the soul balance. You need to understand that too."

John led me to a crystal meditation hall. We sat together. For the next period of time, which was incalculable, I felt myself deep in a "think-sleep" meditational state, a state of consciousness, John said, that was used for learning. Days and weeks and months seemed to pass. Time was not a dimension I recognized anymore. My meditation was timeless.

I sat with John in the lotus position and meditated until I

felt all my seven chakras vibrate with color. He guided my meditation. I felt the vibration of my own spirit until I felt the light of my original auric state of being. I felt close to my divine, angeliclike state. Then I saw, enveloped in a kind of mist, the features of another soul pass across my face. Though I couldn't see who it was, I felt myself make the decision to become a portal for the return of that soul. Soon, through deeper meditation, I materialized my own pregnancy. And when I came out of that nirvanic state, I knew that conception of a physical body had been completed. John said that in the fourth month, the soul of another would enter the new body within me and the child within me would move.

John then said I was ready to participate in a great new experiment in Atlantis that would "improve" the civilization there. He said the Council of Elders in Lemuria, along with the solicited help of the extraterrestrials, had voted democratically to pursue the new experiment, and they all felt that in the Deity's eyes it was necessary. With the Atlantean attraction to technology, the concentration on materialism and "self" was propelling them to pursue egotism and attitudes of superiority. And those attitudes needed to be altered. A fundamental reordering of spiritual priorities in the human being had to be instituted. He said I was one of those who had volunteered to initiate the program that ultimately everyone on earth would be subject to. I was not to speak about it yet because it would only be too disturbing to those who would attempt to understand. I was simply to prepare myself and, when the time came, leave for Atlantis.

Suddenly the scene in Lemuria and the Temple of Learning shifted. I was no longer there. Instead, I stood at the center of a thoroughfare, aware of how harsh the sounds were around me. The buying and selling of goods was evident everywhere. People spoke loudly at the tops of their voices. There had been no voices in Lemuria. Only the powerful transference of thoughts. Smells of food cooking—a kind of fried smell—hung in the air. The perfumed floral scent from Lemuria was gone. As I looked more closely, I noticed that a few people now had either a male or a female form. The women were decorated with gemstones and metal in their ears, around their necks, and on their arms and fingers. Paint adorned their faces, their lips and cheeks. Their voices were high-pitched, and they talked fast. The men, on the other hand, seemed more deliberate, their voices were much lower, more stentorian, and I observed that they often walked in front of the women. They wore no ornaments except for hair on their faces, which surprised me because I had never seen body hair or facial hair in Lemuria.

Like bubbling cauldrons, I noticed disturbances break out intermittently from various corners of the street life. A dog, looking hungry, walked into a circle of squabbling merchants. Someone kicked the dog, who yelped and slunk away with its tail between its legs.

Children played in gangs, laughing harshly. Their body

movements became clandestine when they were aware of an adult in their midst.

There were trees, shrubs, and flowers along the roadways, but the reds weren't as vibrant, and the green of the leaves was olive rather than iridescent.

Moats and fountains and terraces were carved into the hillsides. Spacecraft, piloted by extraterrestrials, hovered near and above the space ports. There seemed to be a distinct separation between the aliens and the earth beings now as they interrelated. As I surveyed the life around me, I looked for John. He was not there. Then I heard someone humming in the distance, and the sound was beautiful to me.

A man walked forward to greet me. I looked into his face. I recognized him as my present-day father! He had dark hair tumbling down his back. We interlocked our palms in greeting, touched our faces cheek to cheek, and walked casually together. I rubbed the center of my forehead and pressed hard. He, of course, didn't know he would be my twentieth-century father. In this lifetime he was apparently a good friend.

He seemed excited as he talked about the new values in Atlantis. But as we walked together, I was aware that his body movements were not liquid and gentle like the movements of the body in Lemuria. He didn't flow as he moved. His gestures seemed jerky and slightly discordant.

"Things are very different here," Dad said. "Some of it is confusing, but to most of us it is extremely exciting."

There was noise as we walked. I realized I was hearing spoken language.

"I see," said Dad, "that you are preparing for birth."

I smiled and touched my stomach. Then I looked into the sky.

"Yes," I said. "I'm preparing a portal for a new life."

I felt a strange twinge of anxiety, but said nothing. Extraterrestrial crafts of all sizes lifted and zoomed through the sky. Alien beings transporting crystal moved everywhere. John had said the extraterrestrials used crystals for thought amplification and highly intense spiritual concentration for the new project.

As Dad and I walked together, I felt myself become slightly confused, as though he and I were thinking separate thoughts instead of harmonious thoughts. I found it difficult to communicate with him.

"Yes," I said. "I can see immediately that Atlantis is different. Why is so much crystal being used?" I wondered if he knew what John had told me.

"There are strange new and wonderful experiments being conducted," he said, "and they use the crystals for them. I'm not sure what they entail. Only those on the highest level participate. But I understand it's been agreed to by all involved as a path toward higher spiritual activity."

I looked at Dad, but said nothing. We walked through the busy, bustling streets. I had not been prepared for the difference in tempo or the differences in physical appearance. There was so much more noise, and everyone moved more quickly with what seemed like slightly disjointed body movements. People were dressed as though done up for a gala, the various distinguishing colors of their turbans, my father explained, denoted their social rank.

"You have social distinctions here?" I asked him.

"Yes," he replied, "that's part of the new way. It's fun to become the most respected color."

"The most respected? What is the system here? It is indeed different."

"Well," said Dad, "at home in Lemuria everything worked communally because everything was spiritually motivated to nourish the collective soul, but here it's more colorful—more multidimensional and individualistic."

"How?" I asked.

"Well, we have the governmental authorities, the literary and intellectuals, the artisans, a limited military that serves as police and sanitation corps, and—"

"Wait," I said. "You have a military and a police force?"

"Yes," said Dad, bright-eyed.

"Why?" I asked.

"Well," said Dad, "because we have so much art and knowledge to protect. We don't want our progress to be infected by crime."

"Crime?"

"Yes, crime."

"What is crime?"

Dad was a little astonished that I seemed so naive. "Well, crime is when an individual commits an act against the law."

"What kind of law?"

"Well, a law made by the government to protect society."

"But whom must you protect society from?"

"Why, from each other," he said.

I sadly remembered John's words. "When a society begins to think separately one from the other, it is the beginning of the end of the civilization," he had said.

I saw now that the buildings here in Atlantis were walled in, and around the larger, more palatial structures were moats. Above the moats, close to the homes, were terraces of earth and clay supporting vegetable life of all kinds.

The entrances to the homes were concealed under rock ledges as though to hide what might be inside. Vines and rock-loving plants hung from the ledges.

"Come to my home first," said Dad. "Rest and meditate, and then you can report to the birthing hall. Is that agreeable?"

I nodded, noticing that it was very difficult for me to talk in a spoken language.

"I live over there," said Dad, "on the middle floor."

I saw a series of vertical verandas with apartment dwellings just adjacent. Enormous vases holding earth and plants of many varieties perfumed the air around the dwelling's entrance. Fountains spraying from below cooled the air with their mist. Above the first story, with its flower-filled verandas, arose another tier of dwellings surrounded by open galleries, the floors of which were formed by the roofs of those beneath. Songbirds and uncaged birds of plumage welcomed us.

"Please, enter," said Dad, gesturing me inside.

I obeyed, bending over slightly in order to clear the top of the entrance. Inside the dwelling a shaded, high-tension, airless cylinder lamp cast a soft glow throughout the interior. Sparse and clearly spartan, the room had no furniture, and marble floors supported meditation mats.

"Make yourself peaceful," said Dad. "I am going out for a moment."

I smiled and said good-bye, and thought of my childbirth plans and what I had committed to.

I sat in the lotus position on one of the thin mats, and within minutes, I was aware of people waiting for me in the birthing hall.

Hurriedly, I left Dad's home, hoping he wouldn't be disappointed at coming home to find me gone.

I noticed many pregnant beings as I made my way through the streets. I wondered how many of them had come to my decision for the improvement of the society.

Long and lithe extraterrestrials came and went in their crafts, which carried great varieties of crystals as well as people. I noticed the crystals in Atlantis were of more multishaped forms.

Somehow I knew where I was going. I stopped in front of

the dome-shaped birthing hall, but understood immediately that I should enter the tall, crystal-shaped pyramid next to it instead. There were no particular markings.

In the crystal entrance chamber I was greeted by three translucent-skinned extraterrestrials and two Lemurians who introduced themselves as genetic engineering code experts. We clasped palms. I nodded my greetings and followed them into a blue mist chamber. Carefully arranged on a marble tabletop stood two life-size crystal shapes outlining each portion of the human frame. I examined the crystal forms closely. They were exquisitely detailed in their carving, from the skulls to the brains to the genitalia. I noticed one was male and one female. I remembered that I had never seen the human genitalia separated into two sexes before. It made me feel strange and rather lonely.

I nodded my head as I fingered the crystal shapes. Two attendants then led me to a crystal tank filled with the same golden liquid I had seen during the birth in Lemuria. I looked down at my stomach, trying to communicate with the new soul I knew now resided there.

A council of elder extraterrestrials, Lemurians, and Atlanteans formed a semicircle on one side of the crystal forms. They greeted me warmly, thanking me deeply for my courage. I responded by giving thanks to the Divine Spirit. I said I understood what I was about to do and said I hoped that I could be of some spiritual service.

The council collectively thanked me again and stood. Then, slowly, ritualistically, they removed their garments as I followed suit. As the council group stood in ceremonial nakedness, half the group was androgynous, the other half not. I entered the crystal tank. The elders sat down.

I stood peacefully in the golden liquid that covered my body. My breathing was even and controlled. Soon I went into deep meditation.

"Let us begin," said the senior member of the council of elders.

They sat in lotus positions around the crystal shapes. Time passed until their frequencies began to vibrate. Soon they were collectively levitating, their chakras totally illuminated and their auras a blazing light. Their light energy increased. A blazing ring of white energy emanated from the group. Then the members of the council transferred their own energy to the crystals. From each individual's third eye in the center of his forehead, a beam of light streaked to the crystal forms on the table.

Then with an accelerated electromagnetic frequency, the beams of light converged and formed arcs of light that leaped from the crystal forms on the table to me in the tank. I felt the collective energy reach me. I knew the moment of my "cooperation" had arrived. I was filled with trepidations, but trustful. There was no turning back now. I arched my body toward the arcs of light as though complying with the will of a higher wisdom. The energy generated began to light the golden liquid in the tank.

Slowly, I felt my body begin to expand around the area of my shoulders, causing them to feel briefly dislocated. There was no pain, just dislocation. I hunched my body forward. I felt a large hump form across my shoulders. The council accelerated their energy from their third eyes. I could feel their power. I relaxed and hunched my body forward even more until slowly it became evident to me that I was forming another spinal column down my back. I breathed more deeply to control my physical fear. In my mind I felt reasonably calm. The separation of my own spinal column was in progress, and it was as though I were watching it happen. At the same time, I involuntarily began an increased heartbeat. I knew I shouldn't attempt a decrease in metabolic pulsation, and soon the rate of acceleration stopped when it was clear to me that I had sustained two pulses and had materialized two hearts.

I then realized the dualization of my other internal organs was clearly in progress. Soon I would be two separate people. Across my chest on the left side, female breasts began to form. On the other side, the chest remained masculine. My thighs began to expand until out of each thigh came two thighs. The two thighs on the masculine side were muscular and firm. On the feminine side they were lithe and slim. The concentrated energy now moved to my stomach—my full and pregnant abdomen. With a gentle undulation, the protruding stomach caved in. Simultaneously, the flat stomach separated, becoming two stomachs, one rounded and feminine, the other muscular and taut. I felt myself go into deeper meditation. It was necessary because there was no way I could relate to what was happening to me. Still, there was no pain, and still, I was trustful.

In my mind's eye I saw my genital area begin to separate. The male genitals went to the male side of the new body and the female to the female side. I felt, even in my think-sleep state, a sharp twinge of alienation, a sensation of anxiety and loss. The council of elders now meditated on the two crystal skulls at the top of the human forms. Their light frequencies accelerated even more. The arcs of light blazed with energy. I bent in supplication until my head touched the arcs of blazing light. When the arcs of light made contact with my head, two heads began to form. I felt my brain swim. I felt I was losing myself and my identity. I felt my features begin to change entirely as my head divided into two. There were no more features of the original me. Instead, my original features melded into the male side of the new head and an entirely new set of features evolved onto the female side of the head. I understood that the soul of the child in my stomach had incarnated into the female form, and the soul of myself came to rest in the male form. Then I saw that my twin soul from Lemuria had returned through my provided portal, but had taken the physical form of a female. My own androgynous soul would now live as a male.

The division of the sexes was nearly complete. But the two

separate bodies were still joined at the ribs. Slowly, the rib joints peeled off and the result was two complete bodies—one male (me) and one female (my twin soul).

Eve being born of Adam's rib was accomplished.

As soon as complete division had occurred, the Council of Elders snapped their energies shut, leaving only their circular aura as an afterglow. They were exhausted and covered in perspiration. But with the collective help, input, knowledge, and expertise from each other and their extraterrestrial brethren, they were beginning a new dawn for the human race—male and female. I lost consciousness. There were no more images.

* * *

I felt the sun shining on my eyes. It was hot and reassuring. I opened them. I was lying in a field in Spain surrounded by cows at some distance. I shook myself awake and climbed from my sleeping bag. I felt my arms and legs and torso. I was in one piece.

I felt my waist and hips and breasts. Yes, I was still a female.

I pulled down my shorts and urinated. Yes, that was still real. I stood up. I blinked into the sun. What had the night-vision meant? I had been divided in two? And then become a male? I remembered John saying that the myth of Eve being born out of the rib of Adam was in so many human cultures because it had in fact been our heritage. That meant our natural state was androgynous because our souls were perfectly balanced yin and yang, positive and negative, masculine and feminine, and the body should reflect the soul. I couldn't compute this in a logical way, yet somehow it felt true. How long ago had this separation of sexes occurred? John had said the whole genetically engineered experiment had taken hundreds and thousands of years.

It was obvious that in the world today most everyone was looking for a companion who might reflect the part of themselves that was missing. That seemed to be the ongoing anxiety of civilization for most people. Songs, literature, novels, jokes, religion, and spiritual searching seemed to be motivated by a desire to find and connect with the missing half of ourselves. Could this division and separation from my original self be what I was looking for? Not so much as a search for a companion but as a reuniting with a balanced spirit that reflected the Deity's Divine Energy?

Balance was the issue: the balance of masculine and feminine in myself, which would reflect the balance and harmony of my soul.

Was this part of what the Buddhists called the "Middle Way"? The consciousness reflecting perfect middle balance of the yin and the yang? As I thought of it, almost every depiction of the Buddha I had seen seemed androgynous. . . .

So sex was not the issue—balance was. And with that balance (which certainly required courage in today's cultures) came the familiarity of the soul's journey. Everything each of our souls had experienced through millions of years was still a part of our genetic memory. We had been both male and female, because in the beginning we were a reflection of the soul that was divinely both.

I stood looking up toward the sun with my eyes closed. Something told me to open them, and I saw a man approaching me. I tried to seem preoccupied with myself. But he walked up to me.

"Good morning," he said. "May I have your autograph?"

17

He said his name was Juan and he wanted to talk to me. I gave the autograph to him, indicated I didn't want to talk, and rolled up my sleeping bag.

He began to talk incessantly, although I did my best to ignore him. He said his brother had been abducted by extraterrestrials and taken away in a UFO. He said the message from them to his brother had been that suffering was a conditioned response that we humans devoutly and profoundly believed we deserved and thought was necessary to human life—but we were wrong. "Suffering was a method of institutionalizing control and was basically a genetic memory that we lived with from the past but wasn't inherent to our genetic makeup." He said,

"If that belief could be erased, there would be no more wars, conflict, killing, or starvation."

I listened with weary ears. Then I looked into his face. "Of course, stupid, but how do we stop it? I don't want to have a conversation with you about karma, UFOs, or life suffering. I wouldn't know how."

"But you know all about those things," he said. "I read all your books."

"I know nothing," I said, hoping to finish him off. "I'm not even sure I'm walking toward Cebreiro right now. Am I?"

"Yes," he answered.

"But am I making it up that I'm walking?"

"What do you mean?" he asked, rightfully confused.

"I don't know what I mean. I don't know what anything means. I'm not even sure I'm alive."

This man, Juan, continued to walk with me. I didn't have the energy to outpace him, so I was condemned to talk to him and try to answer questions. It wasn't long before I gratefully realized that, irrespective of his brother's abduction and the fall from grace of mankind and all the laws of earth-plane suffering and karma, he really wanted to talk about Hollywood anyway. He was very opinionated about Hollywood films being inferior to European films. I found both topics of conversation unfathomable. I walked on up the mountain until I lost him and found myself looking down on a sea of clouds. I remembered my father's advice: "He travels fastest who travels alone."

But what was I traveling toward? And what had I traveled from? What would my dad think of it all?

I had a message from Anna at one of the *refugios*. She was in Santiago waiting for me. Baby Consuelo, the Brazilian singer, was two days behind.

I found another Brazilian woman in the *refugio* whom I had met a few weeks before. She was sick from contaminated water. She was lying next to a man who was also sick. Both were married, but not to each other.

"The Camino worked its magic," she said to me. "I love my husband, but I never felt I needed him. Now I realize I need a man. This affair won't last past the Camino, but when I return to my husband I know I will need him." (She must have been one of the early ones to go through a sexual division in Atlantis, I thought.)

How anyone could find the energy to make love five or six times a day on the Camino while sick was a mystery to me. You had to be sick. Which, of course, she was.

I went out by a stream and read the only book I had—the New Testament. I randomly opened to Matthew 24. And there it was. "And you will hear of wars and rumors of wars . . . for nation will rise against nation, and kingdom against kingdom, and there will be famines and earthquakes. . . ." Were we setting ourselves up for some terrible cataclysm?

I looked up. A helicopter was circling. Oh, God. I knew why. But an aircraft ambush was going a little far.

I fled to a monastery nearby, but I couldn't get in. I was trapped outside. The helicopter landed. I closed my New Testament and stood there, ready for my next revelation. The press piled out of the helicopter and shouted questions at me while rolling their cameras. I stood still and said absolutely nothing. I put myself in another time and place (which wasn't difficult). The press became embarrassed (unique). The priest from the monastery came out finally and let me inside, where I sat staring out at the press for two hours (a nice rest).

The priest then took me out the back door and to a small restaurant.

The press followed me there. They began to provoke me at the dining table, yelling and knocking things over (spontaneous pictures?). I said nothing at all and did nothing, just sat there quietly eating bread. Nice fresh bread. There was no story, there were no quotes, no sound bites, and only boring pictures, in which *they* looked quite vicious (their karma returned to the source?).

I realized now, however, that the press knew I hadn't much further to go to complete the Camino. They would be everywhere. What was I going to do? I was absolutely determined not to give them anything. They could print that I was on a return visit from hell, and I wouldn't care.

At that moment Carlos and Ali, accompanied by *Juan*, walked into the small restaurant. Oh, God, I thought. Who is this Juan? Carlos began to mock-beat at the press with his staff, and Ali screamed at them. It was good to have irate friends. I couldn't muster any anger. But I could see that eluding the press would now be an escape game for me. And, as John the Scot had told me from my previous time on the Camino, I had learned a few tricks from hating to be hunted. Up to now, the press had followed me into church basements where I slept on the floor, invaded my showers in the *refugios*, and taunted me on the streets and in restaurants. Was I nakedly helpless? No, now I was going to have some fun.

Would what should be the spiritual understanding and resolution of a long and arduous pilgrimage back in time now become an adventure of escape from those whose frustrations with me were escalating because I hadn't talked to a single one of them? The villagers had told me that the radio and TV reporters were betting that in the end their silent-film footage of me would be accompanied by an in-depth interview because no one who survived the Camino could resist bragging about it. I wondered if any of them had shared their own inner journeys. And had those journeys mirrored mine?

I was determined to get to Santiago de Compostela uninterviewed and unquoted. And I would not let them deter me from finishing my lessons out of the past.

Juan said he knew a friend of the mayor's who would help. His name was José. We recruited José to meet me at the beginning of each of the next four cities and drive me across. That meant the reporters would have to walk the countryside to find me. Thus, eluding them became a challenge and a game for all of us.

I had 115 kilometers (about 71 miles) to go before I reached Compostela.

Juan called José, who brought his car to the restaurant. I went to the ladies' room, escaped through the back door, and fled to José's car. I introduced myself and thanked him. Carlos and Ali and Juan remained in the restaurant as decoys while José drove me across Sarria. I arranged for him to meet me again before I reached Portomarín.

José let me out, and I got lost again. The yellow arrows looked completely different in that part of Spain. I couldn't find any indications. All I saw were journalists' faces in my mind. I retraced my steps for a few miles. I asked directions from a woman in her house. She screamed at me. I ran. Instead of crying, I became more determined.

I stopped several cars and asked for the Camino arrows. They didn't know what I was talking about. It was as though I were on another planet and the Camino didn't exist. I stopped a man who pulled out a map. He pointed to a church on the map. But in reality there was no church. Then an older lady came up to me. She said I should look for a grove of trees and I would find a yellow arrow on a rock nearby. I thanked her and left. I found the trees, but there were two huge dogs under them. They snarled a warning to me. I couldn't find the arrow. Then the elderly lady called them away. They obeyed her. I found the arrow and followed it. I found an isolated phone booth and called Kathleen again. We talked about her condition, and I said

I was having some disturbing past-life recall. She had been respectful of my searching curiosity, but was fundamentally disbelieving. Then she said something I needed to hear.

"You have always been used to instant comprehension," she told me. "Because you have a sharp mind, these things are difficult for you. But you can't understand everything, now, can you? Isn't that the lesson? Look at me. I don't understand why I'm dying except that my dead husband wants me."

How could I tell her what I was "learning"?

*　　*　　*

I walked until I found a *refugio*. Outside were two men, very angry because they couldn't get in. They wanted water; they wanted to lie down; they were furious. I decided to keep walking.

I could feel myself rushing. When would John come to me again? I wanted to learn and see more, but also I wanted to finish and get off the Camino and out of Spain.

I had left my backpack in the car with José. I thought of things that gave me earth-plane pleasure. I wanted to sit and drink gallons of sweet carbonated sodas. I wanted to stuff myself with seven-course French meals. I had flashes of desire to make outrageous amounts of money so that if I lived to be really old, I'd never have to experience the poverty I saw in the villages I walked through. Yes, I'd make tons of money, and would give most of it to the poor. At the same time I furiously promised myself I would never, never, overeat again; I would always take care of my body because it was my path back to God. I would never mistreat it again, because of what I'd been through; and I would work on my impatience at things I didn't comprehend.

I walked with such haste my ankles became inflamed. There were flowering bushes up ahead swarming with bees. I had no choice but to walk through them. I put my netting over my head, and as the bees swarmed around my face, I walked through nature's terrible beauty.

When I reached the agreed-upon restaurant outside of Portomarín, I found Ali and Juan and Carlos waiting for me. Ali and Carlos had hitched a ride with Juan. José wasn't there, though. And he had my backpack.

Juan was a man who was very negative about everything. His brother had apparently not inculcated him with extraterrestrial positivity. He liked to argue about the sun, the food, the plans. I gently broached the topic of his negativity with him because he was difficult to be around. He agreed and thanked me for pointing it out, going on to say that nowhere in the world were there as many bars with as many people arguing over nothing as in Spain. He said the repression of the Franco fascist government had built up frustrations in people that were now being released. Right. He failed to acknowledge that Franco was twenty years ago. Juan then went to call José. Soon José arrived. I wondered how Juan knew where he was.

José then drove me to Portomarín, where I saw press and

TV cameras waiting for me, unsuspecting that I was in a car. José drove me across the city. I jumped out of the car and continued to walk as the press waited behind me.

The Camino now seemed to be a walking meditation on what I had learned internally. I knew it would be the end of a big part of my life and the beginning of a new one. If there had, indeed, been a time in human history, millions of years ago, when we humans had been more balanced with a sense of divinity, I would endeavor to bring it up from my memory in my everyday life now and use it.

If the Garden of Eden had indeed been lost, I would seek to find it again. If other terrestrial species had sought to achieve that balance themselves, then I would give more attention to UFO sightings and why they were here. And if they were here to help us but first needed to be acknowledged, I would do that too.

And if we had once been androgynous, then I would cease to stereotype any person's sexual orientation or preference. If the Camino's energy had amplified all those memories for me, then I would trust it.

I was walking toward the end of the known world, but I had memories of the unknown one. Perhaps all the saints and sinners and kings and queens and soldiers who had trekked here had these same haunting memories of a time they wished to recapture in themselves. And perhaps none of us wanted our great modern civilization to suffer the fate of those that preceded us.

By now the press was never really sure where I was because of the arrangement I had made with José to drive me across the remaining cities. I had changed my recognizable clothes, buying new ones, and walked without the familiar-looking backpack, which José carried. I wore another new hat, carried my rolled-up sleeping bag, and hoped not to be recognized. José had gotten word that the press was staking out many remaining *refugios*. The pilgrims who were still walking would give them misinformation about my whereabouts. Our cat-and-mouse game now included many more players. When I slept, it was either outside or in a basement of an abandoned church, and never for more than five hours.

In the meantime, a radio and TV report announced that someone walking with me was recording everything we discussed, which their viewers and listeners should stay tuned for.

Ali and Carlos would sometimes appear with José when he met me at the outskirts of a city. They said they didn't trust Juan. They wanted to protect me from him. I wasn't sure. I would wait and see.

It always fascinated me how celebrity stimulated the well-intentioned paranoia of people who saw themselves as friends and protectors of the famous. People seemed to admire that there was a celebrity who truly wished *no* publicity for a change. In every village people began hanging out of windows, yelling *"Ultreya."* The jungle telegraph gave me great emotional support.

When José and I were in the car alone, crossing a city, we talked about life. He asked me why I was making the pilgrimage. I said, "To finish it." He asked if I was Catholic. I said, no, I had my own brand of spiritual worship. He asked me what it was, and in the absence of a logical explanation, I just laughed. I asked him if he was Catholic.

"Oh, yes," he said. "Strict."

"Married?"

"Yes."

"Do you have affairs?"

"Of course."

"Well, what about the rules of the church?"

"They have nothing to do with that part of my life. If I had a beautiful meal placed in front of me, I'd eat it. So if there is a beautiful woman . . . I never lie about what I do. I always tell the truth."

"Do you tell your wife?"

"Of course not. I have two mistresses."

"Oh," I said. "And what are they like?"

"Married," he answered. "Both of them."

"And would you mind if your wife had a lover?"

"No," he said. "I love her."

No wonder the bars were full of people arguing over nothing.

He left me off outside of Arzúa. I didn't have far to go— less than twenty-five miles to complete the Camino to Santiago. It was now July 2, and I hadn't been in contact with John the Scot since my night in the field. I couldn't remember how many days ago that had been. I was in another time zone. I barely knew where I was.

At the end of the day I found an abandoned *refugio*. It smelled of musty memories . . . yes, memories had now taken on a smell to me. In fact, I almost felt I could hear color and see sound by now.

I opened the creaking door. Broken-down bunks stood like empty, lonely erector sets. One double-decker had a top bunk that still had springs. I crossed the filthy floor, which must have been trodden on by many blistered feet. My blisters were now of insignificant concern to me. Two mice scampered in front of me.

I climbed to the top bunk and unrolled my sleeping bag. I untied my boots, took them off, and hung them safely by their laces.

As I crawled into my bag, fully clothed and as filthy as the *refugio,* I fell asleep. I knew that John would come again because I was taking my time and unconcerned about the press. They would never look for me here.

As I slipped into sleep consciousness, I let myself go.

Through the familiar tunnel of light I raced until I found myself once again in the crystal pyramid in Atlantis.

18

The misty crystal chamber swam back into focus in front of my mind. I became consciously aware of a warm, golden liquid surrounding me in the crystal tank. I remembered that I had just completed the sexual division and was now looking at the separation from myself. And I remembered I was now only a male. My eyes felt strange to me. I moved my torso. I felt a dull throb, but nothing more. I tried to smile, but felt too unfamiliar with my body. I floated—I knew that—I floated, and when I looked over at the new body next to me, I knew she recognized me. I choked back a gasp. I looked down at her genitals and then at my own. My female half was now missing.

Since half of myself was missing, I felt unwhole physically. I couldn't really say it was a mental feeling. In fact, mentally and spiritually, I felt fine because my soul and spiritual feelings were androgynous anyway. That was fundamental: basic, inherent, intrinsic, primeval, primitive—true and natural. But suddenly I was more aware of my physical body than I had been in Lemuria, and because of the division, I felt an inability to adjust to incompleteness. I felt myself desperate to be with my partner in the tank. It was the other half of me; she was my twin soul. I wanted to know what my twin soul felt, what she thought, what she felt about me. I wanted to *be* her in a way that meant I wanted to be totally myself again. I wanted to possess her as though I wanted to be in possession of myself again. I wanted to control her in the same way I wanted to have complete mastery over myself. I felt confused. I communicated those feelings to the Council of Elders, who responded that they understood and it was not unusual. I questioned how I should proceed. They answered that I should have patience.

My twin-soul partner was not only exhausted beside me, but also I felt her soul to be open-eyed and completely astonished by her new environment and body. She was, I reminded myself, after all, a soul newly reincarnated into a fully adult, materialized human female. She would have to adjust to her new three-dimensional physicality and her own limitations of being only female, as I was only male.

She limply smiled at me as several attendants lifted us gently from the tank. She seemed completely out of touch with the idea of having a body. Her skin was a golden honey color, her eyes big and brown, and her facial bone structure finely chiseled. Her hair was a dark chocolate, and around her mouth was a strong-boned chin line. She was the twin soul who had willingly "died" in the birthing tank in Lemuria and whom I would later meet on the Camino as Charlemagne in 790 A.D. and who would later become Olaf Palme in the twentieth century.

The attendants gently lifted and placed us onto crystal carts. The carts rolled side by side, so each of us was in the company of the other, moment by moment. I reached out my new and unfamiliar arm to her. She took my hand. She felt warm and comforting and soft to me. I felt protected by her warmth and softness. I felt it was safe to be vulnerable with her. I felt that she would provide me with all the qualities I somehow felt I lacked myself. I felt I would make her a very good mate also.

The two of us were gently rolled into a crystal scanning room, where attendants screened our bodies for defects with crystal screens. There were none. The division had apparently been successful. Now we would go through a program for sexual adjustment.

After an indeterminate time of peaceful rest, healing musical chords, deep meditation, soothing oil massages, and collective energy supplies from the Council of Elders, she and I began our program in what would come to be known as tantric exercises. From the moment of division we had never been apart. We were aware that we were twin souls and totally compatible as a result, and we were told by the council that the twin-soul system was basic to pairing for the sexual division of the Lemurian culture. In that way the adjustment to sexual division would only really be a physical adjustment, and the sexual ecstasy that would potentially occur between us had never been experienced by humans up to that point before. With sexual pairing, the soul children could go forth and multiply, providing the Deity with more entities who could bear witness to it and thereby fulfill themselves and their own struggle for divinity.

She and I were taken to a new chamber, where we would be completely alone to discover ourselves and each other, after having had a simple outline of physical instruction.

Although we were adult and mature after division, we were essentially sexual virgins. We both had had the experience of undergoing pregnancy, but we had, of course, never expressed ourselves sexually before. We had been androgynous beings with no sexual stress systems built in in order to cope with the complexities. So tantra was designed for those original adult beings with no sexual consciousness.

We were told that the purpose of sexuality was to cause and create intimacy with another human being so that each would understand that no one was an island. Sexuality was to be specifically the dialogue—telepathically, hormonally, spiritually—

between two beings through the seven chakras (which were energy centers and organs of the soul) and all the physical and mental senses, with the explicit purpose of causing intimacy.

Sexuality was to be the language to remerge the souls. And the physical attractiveness would be the motivating factor in each being reexamining himself.

Sexuality, we were told, was to put one in closer contact with the Deity, because when one was intimately involved with another human being, one was closer to the Divine, since that other person was another part of the Divine.

She and I found ourselves in a room bathed with a misty violet glow. In the center of the room was a sunken tub containing warm, oily water. We were told that the slippery, oily-textured liquid was a natural extension of the fluids of the human body during male–female sexuality.

The tub itself was made from a form-fitting papyrus substance and kept the oil within it warm.

We quietly lowered ourselves into the slippery, caressing water, and quickly realized that it was very deep.

From our earlier Lemurian training and complete mastery of our previous bodies, we understood that by a deep intake of oxygen and a deliberate slowing of the metabolic pulse rate, we would be able peacefully to contemplate each other with X-ray clairvoyance under the water. The physical auras of each of us would be more visible under the oily water because the liquid acted as an energy conductor.

We took a deep breath of oxygen, touched each other's palms, and gently holding palms, we sank to the bottom of the deep tub. What followed occurred over a period of some months. We observed the tantric exercises every day.

We assumed the lotus position and began to gaze tenderly at each other. We were aware that we should concentrate on our outer physical forms. So we began slowly to absorb visually our two new bodies. Beginning at our heads, we isolated each other's hair, eye color, nose shape, mouth curvature, and neck length. As we isolated each feature simultaneously, we each noticed that the chakras of the other were lighting up.

I concentrated on her heart area. I could see the green aura of the heart chakra shimmering in the energized water. Her heart seemed to have a color and frequency all its own. I was aware that my own frequency was similar to hers. I found the vibrational similarity very attractive and wanted to confirm my satisfaction by touching her, but my instructions had been to wait. To wait until I had made myself familiar with each isolated physical part of her and she, likewise, of me.

As I progressed down her body, I became aware that there was an increased blood flow to each internal organ that I isolated, almost as though the organ itself reacted to the attention. We each discovered the same thing in the other.

The two of us would sit and gaze peacefully at each other under the oily water. Because of our historical practices in prana breathing techniques, the Council of Elders told us that our lungs had a very large capacity for oxygen and could sustain a great deal of hemoglobin. They said that because we were such tall people, there was more blood to fill our large frames, thereby enabling the storing of more oxygen. Our hearts beat at a rate of one heartbeat per minute because of the psychic peacefulness, and the slow metabolic rate was the reason why we didn't age. The teachers reminded us that we had learned to master our bodies completely—heart, lungs, liver, pancreas, pineal, pituitary glands, and so on—that all children had been taught such techniques from birth the way today we teach our children to master only their kidneys and bowels. Lemurians gave their children crystal toys shaped into parts of the human anatomy so they would understand their bodies in relation to pleasure. They didn't believe, they said, in useless toys. Everything they did related to knowledge of themselves and the Deity, and the children derived joy from learning.

She and I saw the sensual clarity in the smooth water as our wide-open eyes began to make clairvoyant contact. We concentrated on raising our vibrational energies in our chakras. We began to spiritualize our bodies through our soul organs.

Slowly I became aware of the blood flow to her female genitals. And as she responded to what she saw, I felt my own blood flow increase. It was difficult for me to isolate whether the blood flow came from feeling the attraction, or whether the attraction came from feeling the blood flow. In either case, it was pleasant and reassuring. I felt the need to feel her, to caress her, to encourage her, and to open her so that I could enter her. I felt an intimacy so pure that I was aware of every aspect of her. I was not only sensitive and aware of her physical surface aspects—such as her eyes, her face and skin, but also her inner physical aspects—her chakras and energy centers. All seven of them were glowing with light, the lower pelvic chakra pulsating in accordance with the higher chakras. The council had explained that all energy emanated from the heart chakra and it was the stabilizing balance so as to sustain a spiritual regulation with the attraction of sexuality. I looked back and forth between her heart chakra and her pelvic chakra. Each gave me as much pleasure as the other, and the combination of the two was ecstasy for me.

The council had said that the entire body was an erogenous zone because the definition of *erogenous zones* was "those isolated areas of sensitivity that corresponded to areas of the body where the personality needed spiritual improvement." In other words, they said that if an area of my body responded to sexual stimulation, it was because that area needed spiritual attention and the corresponding blood flow would help effect that improvement; therefore, the sexual process would be beneficial to my spiritual as well as my physical health. It would not only help ease and release tension but actually treat my entire system when applied spiritually. They said that sex would spiritualize my biological personality because of the use of vibrational energy.

As the weeks and months passed, I became more intensely aware of her. I felt her begin to surrender herself. My own sense of identity began to meld into hers until it seemed to me that a new identity of "oneness" was forming between the two of us. I reached out and touched the palm of her hand. The two of us opened our two palms and gently slid them down the length of our bodies. The electricity I felt was beyond anything spontaneously physical that I had ever known. I felt myself lift out of myself along with her until we seemed mutually sustained by our joint energies. Again, I felt I wanted to *be* her because I wanted to experience that other half of myself that she had become.

I could feel us both abandon our own wills to the will of the process we were experiencing. Neither of us had known spontaneity before, because having been androgynous, we had been totally aware of our own predictable reactions all the time. Sex, then, was our first adventure in spontaneity. It required trust and surrender and a complete spontaneous willingness to give ourselves up to the other person. We felt involved with timelessness. There was a kind of floating, peaceful, nonurgency about our need to have each other. We trusted that we needed no "purpose" in our attraction. That it was, in fact, its own purpose. And the equal sharing of adoration made us feel the Divine.

Then, after some months, we embraced; our arms entwined around one another. I felt myself sigh with deep relief. It was as though I was embracing that part of myself I had loved and lost.

Slowly, she inched her lower pelvis smoothly toward me. I lifted her onto my lap, and she surrounded me with her legs. I responded by drawing her nearer to me. Then we each gently caressed the eyes, the ears, the lips, the hair, the neck, the torso, and the hips of the other—until almost without effort or intention, she opened her legs and I entered her. Neither of us moved. There was no thrust and receive, only gentle pulsation and expanding and retracting. We were lost in each other: she surrounded me, and I was filled. Our physicality seemed to operate as its own process now without our mental motivation. We were experiencing personality surrender for the first time. A larger, more powerful force was carrying us aloft as we succumbed to the cosmic mystery of it.

Then, without intention, purpose, or effort, we each experienced our first sexual release—the release of physical tension brought on by the combustion of fully opened and shared feelings. We actually saw the sparks of energy created by our mutual orgasms. We felt our sparks touch the Divine. We felt spiritually and physically fused. We each poured life into the other and reached a kind of divinity.

I remembered the teachings of John. I remembered how he had said that even though the androgynous Lemurian was highly developed but essentially *self*-contemplative, *self*-concerned, and *self*-spiritualized, and even though the yin and the yang were perfectly balanced within the being, the Lemurians were basically serving the needs of *them*selves. He had said the separation of the

sexes, then, was to be a final test in overcoming the *self*ish identity of *self*-containment. It was an opportunity to improve the
race, through free will, by creating a way to serve an individual
other than oneself. Through sexual division, one had the opportunity to serve another who had distinctly different needs, the
needs of the female being distinctly different from the needs of
the male. Instead of self-service in the androgynous state, we
were creating the opportunity to serve each other, on a physical
and personality level; but on the spiritual level, we were to continue to maintain our androgynous states of mentality.

If the human being learned to serve, he would also be serving the Divine, and with the separation of the sexes into two
beings, the Creator would therefore have more beings to bear
witness to it. The male and female were to go forth and multiply, thereby allowing the opportunity for more souls to incarnate
on the physical plane, which would provide them a vehicle for
working through their karma back to the Divine state of being.

I and my twin soul began to understand our tasks of separate sexualities. We loved each other from the past and were
spiritually evolved enough in the present to remember. As a
result of division, we desperately needed each other.

Our sexual experience was blissful. Our sensual experience
was a joy. Our attraction of opposites was new, fresh, and exciting. Life on the purely physical plane became attractive to us.

And so we two original Lemurians had now become part
of the new Atlantean civilization.

✳ ✳ ✳

We began our life as man and wife in a spartan home with a soothing environment. We listened regularly to healing musical sounds, meditated for long hours in concert with one another, and further developed our tantric knowledge of sexuality.

We loved and lived for one another, reveling in our new discoveries of sexual atonement. Neither of us had the inclination to experiment with anyone else of the opposite sex. The Council of Elders had explained that a monogamous marriage was necessary to our spiritual growth and service to the Creator. Our marriage was, in fact, a spiritual contract observing monogamy as a basic promise. Its purpose was to screen out the idle noise and chatter of the culture that was devolving around us. Total sharing and knowledge of one another was our task in order to bear complete witness to the Deity. Two souls sharing common backgrounds and experiences were to make one experience out of the marital state. The council had explained that every human after division would basically and fundamentally long for one single other soul with which to share all life totally, because we would really be searching for the other half of ourselves. In addition to that, they said the task of each human being was to find its actual soul mate. That would only occur when each human had totally found himself. One could only recognize one's soul mate when one recognized oneself. A soul mate, then, was simply the reflection of one's self.

Thus, there were now two basic motivations that would propel the human race forward. One would be the need for each person to find the counterpart of one's *original androgynous self in another*. The second would be to search for one's original soul mate in spirit. Then, and only then, would one be able to return to the Creator and achieve at-one-ment, thus returning to our original divinity. The council said the human race would be feeling the effects of sexual division throughout eternity, but that it was necessary in order to struggle back to the Divine.

We happily followed the spiritual instructions of the Council of Elders and the extraterrestrials. We both understood that our original soul mates were somewhere else. Soon she became pregnant and gave birth to a baby boy, thus establishing ongoing sexual division and also her lineage, which would follow down through the ages. We were perfect partners for each other, and together we became more and more knowledgeable. In fact, soon we became completely obsessed by knowledge ... knowledge of technology, knowledge of art, knowledge of literature (we were now using only spoken language).

But my partner and I found that the more we and the rest of Atlantean civilization became involved with information and knowledge (which we found extremely attractive), the more we were drawn away from our spiritual purpose.

With the growing emphasis in Atlantis on the material and physical planes, and with the gradual disintegration of spiritual knowledge and spiritual reverence, we began to lose our spiritual identities. We became totally involved in our male and female identities. We developed male and female ego structures and lost touch with our true androgynous souls and spiritual selves. In becoming totally seduced by earth-plane values, by the material and physical pleasures of the flesh, and by the intellectual rather than the spiritual aspects of life, we, along with others we knew and communicated with, began to devolve. We, as Atlanteans who had agreed to sexual division, could have taken a dramatic step forward in our own evolution to perfection, but once again, we failed. We could have accomplished the final test in the evolution of our divinity, but instead we made the same mistake that we made originally as soul forms—we became sensually seduced by the physical and abandoned our divine origins. The extraterrestrials had used their psychic and genetic technologies to help accelerate the evolution of the lower primates into the Adamite race, and now they had tried to help accelerate the process of realized divinity by sex division. Perhaps they would be more successful when mankind itself was ready.

For now, the Adamite race was cast out of the Garden of Eden, having eaten of the tempting fruit of the Tree of Knowledge.

But as I turned away from spirituality, I became, for the first time, an emotional being. For until then, I, as an androgynous human, had been a sensitive being but not emotional.

I had never cried, for example, because there was nothing

to cry about. I had known no such thing as the fear of death because there was no such thing as death, only physical termination of the body. I had had relationships, but no emotional attachments because I had been attached only to the Deity. I had had no sexual attachments because there was no need for sex, since I was self-contained.

I had had no partner, no mate, no husband, no wife. I had had no identity confusion because the yin and the yang in my personality had been balanced. That, indeed, was the reason I had reached such a high level of spirituality.

I hadn't functioned on a level of logic, but more on a level of sensitivity. I hadn't had emotional concerns, but more sensitive feelings. I had had puzzlements, but no anxiety.

I had been a basically playful being with a great degree of joyous humor. Humor had been the release for tension relating to growth. My humor had never been based on the misfortune of another. The concept was alien to me.

In general terms, I had had feelings, but not emotionality. But now, I began to be aware of profound and fundamental psychological shifts in myself and in the civilization and behavior patterns of the people around me. We all began to feel extremely alienated from the community and each other. We also felt alienated from ourselves. We felt the pain of human emotionality for the first time.

The trauma of the loss of our spirituality caused us to become out of touch with God and with the divineness in ourselves.

From our confusion, a violence seemed to develop. We began to feel frustrated and anxious . . . then angry. We were not even sure what we were angry about—but somehow we were angry at ourselves. Losing touch with the Creator, our own divinity, and the activity of spiritualization, we felt deep emotional conflicts. Conflicts not only deep and disturbing, but conflicts that needn't even exist. For to be in tune with the divine was a peaceful and serene state of being. Without the recognition of the Divine Force on a day-to-day basis, we inheritors of the new and modern civilization were rendered helpless to deal with the unnecessary human conflicts we had created by forgetting our original purpose. We grew intensely confused.

Our family life grew increasingly difficult because each of our individual conflicts interreacted with the conflicts of the other. The polarization of our two sexes became more and more evident. Sexual fear and hostility began to develop . . . a kind of fear and hostility neither of us had ever been acquainted with before. And rather than recognition and respect for the divineness in each other and the actual divineness in ourselves, we focused instead on our conflicts and differences. Our small family became the focus and source of more emotional negativity, intensity, and confusion. Our son became as confused and anxious as we were. I began to speculate, wondering if the emotional intensities and confusions would be handed down from generation to generation. If our sins as parents would continue to be visited on our offspring, until our own children would have desperate problems in searching for mates of their own. I noticed that with the loss of spiritualization came an unbridled fear of death and the chilling recognition of mortality. With the absence of spiritual knowledge, I began to fixate on that half of myself that was missing. Having forgotten the Creator, I therefore began to feel half-dead, half-realized, half-complete, half-fulfilled, half-alive. My previous experience of complete self-identity was cut in half. I was now continually searching for a kind of fulfillment from my other half. All of those half feelings contributed to my fear of mortality.

I remembered John had said that out of the loss of spirituality, the fear of death, the trauma of sexual division, and the rise in human conflict, man would become violent, competitive, corrupt, and murderous. I could feel those emotional conflicts happening in me. I felt myself becoming fearful, alienated, and humanly primitive.

I forgot that my purpose was to evolve the divinity in myself.

Though I had committed myself to Atlantis and the test of the new world, after division I could feel myself failing the great human test. Though I knew my responsibility was to my promised commitment to the Divine Deity and to my family, I convinced myself that my life in Atlantis had fulfilled its purpose, that it had no more meaning.

I—in fear, anxiety, conflict, and total alienation from my own spiritual meaning—decided to return to my old world, to my motherland, to my teacher, John . . . to Lemuria. I, therefore, deserted my partner. I left her, my family, my promise, and even my purpose.

I returned to the motherland to find it in a state of devolvement on a par with Atlantis's. The values of the new world had filtered back to the Lemurian motherland, just as John had said. The collective spirituality was disappearing. There was complete division of purpose and thought. Debates raged. Selfishness infected every stratum of the society, which before did not even have strata. Egotism and superiority transgressed the spirituality.

The Garden of Eden was no more. Man had destroyed its harmony.

And with the destruction of spiritual harmony, the ecological harmony disintegrated, for they had always been harmoniously connected. The collective distortion of the electromagnetic frequencies caused by our behavior affected the earth patterns themselves, for the earth was a living organism reacting to the feelings and behavior and treatment of the human family. Meditational nourishment no longer existed as it had previously. The human was alienated from the earth on which it lived. The collective distortion of electromagnetic emotional frequencies caused the earth itself to react—to rebel. To protest. And it did.

After five hundred thousand years of a magnificent civi-

lization, the earth's support system said enough. Due to astro-
nomical and astrological gravitational pulls and also because the
psychic frequencies of the earth's people were not harmoniously positive enough to resist, the earth collapsed. It was the
Deity's way (nature's way) of purging distortion.

During the planet alignments that had occurred every
6,666 years, the earth had resisted the gravitational pulls safely
because it had had psychic and harmonious electromagnetic
support from the higher beings. But now, with the disintegration of human harmony, the living organism called earth had
no higher support system. The magnetic frequencies of the land
and mountains and volcanoes became distorted. The fragile balance between land and mental energies became seriously dis-
rupted. So when the planet alignment occurred, the earth
harmonies collapsed into earthquakes and tidal waves. The
earth needed the help of the Creator's cocreators, the human
family, but we had forgotten our purpose and energy, caught up
in our own distortions.

On returning to my motherland, I saw the horror and disintegration affecting my beloved society. Confusion and corrup-
tion reigned. When the earth itself reacted and the earthquakes
rumbled, when the tidal waves surged, when the great communities toppled and crumbled, I committed a grand sin.

The vulnerable continent of Lemuria sank into the Pacific
like an aging dinosaur, troubled and unable to fend for itself any

longer, forsaken of its human energy, starving and thirsty for its life source and the spiritual electromagnetic frequencies that had nourished her in the past.

I watched Lemuria die; I watched my teacher die, and with a final act of karmic self-destruction, I killed myself.

❊   ❊   ❊

But mine was not a simple suicide. I projected my soul into the astral plane and left my new body behind, my silver cord of attachment intact. I watched the cataclysm below. As millions of people died, I saw their souls collectively depart the earth plane. I felt helpless, unable to serve anyone. Other souls passed me on their journey to higher astral worlds. Desperately, I reached out.

"Wait," I heard myself scream. "Wait. I want to go with you."

And when I experienced the soul of my teacher, John, drifting upward and past me, his body crushed under the pillars of the Temple of Learning below, I panicked in distress.

My teacher had accepted his karmic timing. He had resisted the temptation of astral projection. Experiencing the cataclysm had been his karmic duty, and he knew it. He knew he should maintain a sense of detachment so as to keep an objective viewpoint of his lifetime. His karma was to complete his life cycle. That was everyone's karma. But I refused to confront the reality of the horror below. I found it too painful. My body hadn't yet actually died. My body lay intact below, as yet unaffected by the collapse of the land around me. But the fear and the loneliness of the terror was more than I could cope with. I experienced a sense of guilt I had never felt before. In a desperate attempt to follow my teacher upward to a higher and more spiritual plane, I severed my silver cord and committed an astral suicide. I fully expected to travel upward, following the path of my teacher, but I didn't. Instead, I began to tumble about in space. Everything went black as the spiritual amnesia took effect. I went into a comatose state. Once again, I became an androgynous spirit.

Through time and space I tumbled . . . tumbled . . . tumbled. I felt lost and without a horizon. I felt a frightening kind of limbo. I felt I had lost myself. I felt without purpose, without meaning, without definition. After what seemed an eternity, I awoke on an astral plane. I found myself at a large crystal table. Towering above me was the archangel Michael and his soul mate, archangel Ariel. Their astral wings quivered with high electromagnetic frequencies, and they were benevolent in their attitude, but extremely firm and displeased with me.

The archangel Ariel spoke. As it did, I recognized the vibration in the voice. It was the same sound I'd heard when Ariel had come to me a few weeks back on the Camino. Now I realized that Ariel and the other three archangels were androgynous and Ariel had been guiding me for a long time. The angel spoke to me again now.

"Lemuria," said angel Ariel, "or the Garden of Eden, was a state of balanced consciousness. The individual souls lived for harmony until they partook of the tree of the knowledge of good and evil and rejected the Divine Deity and their spiritual selves. With the development of the ego, they were divided among themselves. You may perceive yourselves as separate, but it is not so. You are benevolent when you desire harmony and love. When you learn to love the Divine Deity with all thy heart and with all thy mind and thy neighbor as thyself, you will kindle in yourself and each other the telepathic energy to heal and protect your collective consciousness from harm. For the soul motivates everything. The soul motivates the natural environment. That soul *is* all. You must achieve that which you really are—a divine soul incarnate in the flesh. Remember the lesson of Lemuria, and perhaps someday you can help restore a once and future Eden to the planet."

Ariel stopped and looked down at me closely, towering above me. I felt totally insignificant.

"The inevitability of your debt is more important than punishment," Ariel said. "You carried out your promise of division. You created a new family. Your family members depended upon you. Your karmic purpose was not yet fulfilled in Atlantis when you chose to depart. It is a karmic crime to depart the physical plane before your time. You are not the judge."

I listened to the judgment of Ariel with profound shame. At the same time, I felt I didn't quite understand.

"In your case," the angel went on, gesturing to indicate the collective decision of the other archangels, "you are forbidden reincarnation until the end of the Atlantean civilization, at which time you will be reborn to serve the future of mankind. After that, you will continue to remain earthbound until after the end of the Adamic Age at the turn of the twenty-first century, at which time you will decide how much longer you want to remain in the body."

"We never punish," Ariel said. "Each individual soul punishes itself."

I saw a golden light envelop Ariel, which expanded to include me. As the light swelled, I understood the words more clearly.

Ariel seemed to become a golden womb enveloping me as I transformed. The angelic wings of Michael expanded to cover both Ariel and me. I felt myself spiritually assume the fetal position until I felt literally reduced to a small infant.

I was sealed and protected in the golden womb of Ariel.

"And when you return to Atlantis to play out your karma, in the civilization you deserted, you will help construct a monument to the preservation of records and knowledge. You will help with the construction of a scenario for the human race. You will help to construct a Bible in stone. It will be a cosmic instrument. Instructions for its use will be carved in gold and placed as wall coverings. We pray the wall coverings will remain intact. Because of its displacement of cosmic energy, it will be used as a communication tool for beings who travel the stars. Earth masters will train within it. It will be located at the epicenter of earth's land mass in Egypt. At this location it should be free from the cataclysmic events that occur every 6,666 years. Within this pyramidal structure will be a record of humanity's past, present, and future events. It will, in effect, be a cosmic time machine. It will serve as a reminder that without spiritual understanding, humankind is doomed. You will serve as one of its architects for the future of humanity. Thus will your karmic debt be paid."

Ariel's enveloping womb gave me warmth and a feeling of emotional support as the words rang in my ears.

Then I felt I began to tumble—an ethereal tumble in space—on my own, but knowing that Ariel was with me.

I looked below me. Lemuria was gone, disappearing under the waves of what is now the Pacific. Millions of souls were surrounding me, floating upward, having accumulated their own individual karma. I wondered if Ariel or Michael spoke to each of them. There was no way of knowing. Each of us had our own individual relationship with the Deity, and to judge would be to do so without the complete knowledge of who each soul actually was.

I began to understand the true meaning of "Judge not, that ye shall be not judged."

The ocean below me surged and fell, surged and fell. I felt myself tumbling again in a kind of limbo. Then, as though through a protective tunnel, I felt myself racing into the present until I was specifically aware that once again I was lying on the top bunk in an abandoned *refugio* in a village in northern Spain.

19

A surge of loneliness rippled through me. I knew it was because what I had experienced would be incomprehensible to anyone I shared it with.

I put on my boots, climbed down from the bunk, rolled up my sleeping bag, and walked outside.

I needed to feel pebbles and earth beneath my feet. I wanted rain on my eyelids and maybe even mosquitoes to shock me back to the reality of the world.

What was the meaning of the reality I had created for myself? Why had I walked the Camino with such perseverance and determination? Had the ancient pilgrims been as obsessed as I? Were we nothing but spiritual overachievers? Was my curiosity about personal identity so intense that I saw more than I could assimilate and process? Had my soul begun with whispers to my mind and now was using a cosmic shout?

I walked faster, pulling some nuts and dried fruit from my waist pack. I fingered the gold cross and breathed deeply. Now all I wanted was to finish the trek.

At the outskirts of the next town (I didn't even know where I was), I was to meet José.

Suddenly, a car pulled up beside me. Alarmed, I looked over at it. Anna was inside.

"You have a plane to Madrid tomorrow night," she said. "The fourth of July. And expect the press on the Mount of Joy, which overlooks Compostela. If you don't want them, elude them."

She laughed and sped off.

I walked further until I spotted José in his car waiting for me. I ran to him and climbed in. "We are to wait for Juan and Carlos and Ali here," he said. I nodded. I told him I was tired so that I wouldn't have to talk to him, and I fell asleep with my face looking up at the sky. When I woke, José said we had waited for Juan and Ali and Carlos for three hours. Three precious hours, when I could have been walking toward Compostela.

"Let's go to the next meeting place," I said finally. We drove in silence. I saw some press and ducked out of sight. When we arrived at the *refugio,* I realized there had been a misunderstanding. They were waiting for us *there.*

Juan was furious. "Well," he said, "I have here your yogurt, your orange soda. Why were you so unclear about where we were to meet?"

That set off Ali. "You are so arrogant," she yelled at him. "I told you we were the wrong distance from town."

"I did not," Juan yelled back at her, using a non sequitur I didn't understand.

They argued in ways I couldn't keep up with. (I wondered if they had been man and wife in Atlantis.)

Finally José chimed in. "Let's calm ourselves. We must get the best out of every day, not the worst."

We sat and ate yogurt, bread, cheese, and almonds.

Juan could not let himself relax with the conclusion that everything had been a misunderstanding. He continued to babble on about who was right and who was wrong. Then he took the burden of it completely upon himself. He walked away, leaned up against a tree, and said, "All of this is too much for me. Too much in one day. You are a celebrity, and I'm suspected of being a spy, then suspected of going to the press, then suspected of taping your conversation. It's all my fault that we wasted your precious three hours. But if you hadn't decided to elude the press, it wouldn't have happened."

No one had accused him of anything. We all stared at him. He had just hung himself out of guilt.

"All right," I said, "let's not talk about it anymore."

Juan went on. "You think I'm arguing all the time, yes?"

"Yes," I said. "So let's stop. It's over." I went into the *refugio* and washed my underwear and socks in the bathroom sink.

Juan followed me in there. "I am a perfectionist," he said.

Ali followed him. "No, a perfectionist is someone who is obsessed with being perfect."

"No," said Juan. "A perfectionist is someone who *is* perfect."

I walked outside and hung my wet clothes on the window-sill of José's car. They all followed. A debate ensued between them over what "perfect" meant.

Finally, I said, "Look, we're all learning lessons about ourselves here. The world is made up of every possible kind of personality imaginable. Don't you think the Camino magnifies all the things in each of us that we haven't yet realized?"

They stopped talking. If only they had understood what I meant.

"Yes, I feel that way," said Ali.

"I'm used to it," said Juan.

"Let's move ahead," said Carlos.

"Let's get in my car," said José. "Juan, take your car alone."

"I'm going to walk alone," I said. "I need to think."

They all piled into José's car. I watched them take off, seeing my underwear flap in the wind from the window as they sped off, their voices echoing more argument in the hot Spanish air.

I smelled terrible; my face was mottled with sunburn; my nails were cracked and peeling; my arms, hands, legs, and face were covered in bites from critters and insects not known to me even in the unknown world. The roots of my hair had grown out two inches. My feet were hooves, and my left eye was red and infected. I was alone again, but strangely happy.

I just kept walking—all the rest of the day. In the night I rested for a few hours by a wide road under trees, press-free. Sleep was no longer necessary anyway, because some kind of "happy completion" endorphins had kicked in. The only thing necessary to me was water. In order to elude the remaining press, I would have to walk nonstop until I got to Santiago. I decided not to stop at the Mount of Joy, which had a *refugio* that looked over Santiago and which was named for the pilgrims' profound joy on reaching the height from which Compostela could first be glimpsed. The joy of the end of their journey. I was going to deny myself that joy because, frankly, I didn't feel it. Not the kind of joy that people spoke of. I felt something I couldn't define . . . a kind of "knowing." I knew somehow that my journey would *begin* at the end of this one. Then I remembered that Anna had said, "The real journey begins when you have processed what you learned from the Camino."

So I continued to walk in a state of determination from which I would not be deterred. I would follow my timetable, arriving on the day of American liberation. Maybe even before. I was certainly still my mother's daughter.

✳   ✳   ✳

The closer to Compostela I got, the more difficult it was to find the arrows. It was also difficult to find the reason for that.

The press thought I was one day behind.

The Camino led under a bridge where the dung was four inches deep. They say that the spiritual road becomes deeper when you wade through negativity, and more narrow when you come closer to your truth.

Wouldn't it be a laugh on me to find that my dream-visions had not been my imagination, but had in fact been the Big Truth. I was living in a world that would laugh at that, but in "reality," was the laugh on them? Were the skeptics the wacky ones?

Were the scientists and intellectuals who needed proof of all matters really the retarded minds among us, because they were threatened by the truth in themselves, wherein lay all the answers they were searching for? Science existed basically as a search for God and the beginning. The church existed basically as the arbiter between man and God. Did the real answers lie within each of those individual souls, who were resistant to looking within for fear of being considered self-centered?

As I walked through the deep dung, I knew that nothing

was more important than looking within, being centered in myself. In my introspection I had revealed to myself some truths I couldn't previously have imagined. I wondered now if I'd allow myself to deeply believe those truths. Or would I allow myself to obfuscate the truth I was seeking? Would I now identify with my multidimensional self as I walked? Would I let myself be those "selves" when I completed the Camino?

I wiped the dung from my boots, having reached the other side of the bridge. I heard Carlos's voice. He was running toward me, waving.

"The press," he yelled excitedly. "They are up there. We can't figure out how they knew. Was it Juan? José?"

He grabbed me and led me in the opposite direction, where we caught the road again. José waited in his car. Carlos pushed me into the car, and José drove me past the press and let me off again.

I ran. I ran until I came to a small bar. I went in to think. How was I going to avoid the press at the Mount of Joy and walk until I reached Compostela? I asked for an orange soda. Then I turned around. There was Juan. Oh, God, he had been the one. He spoke.

"I told the press," he said. "I told the press that you didn't want your picture taken because you believed it would rob your soul."

Jesus, I thought. I could see the headlines now.

Juan turned away, and I sneaked out the back door of the bar.

I fled again. José still had my backpack, so it was easier to move quickly. Up ahead I saw a familiar figure. It was Consuelo, the Brazilian singer. I caught up with her. She said her feet had healed, and she was moving fast. She said she and her husband had decided not to divorce (I didn't know it was an issue). As we ran, we caught up on news of the other pilgrims. She sympathized with my press problems. She said she hadn't gotten any of my messages at the *refugios'* guest books.

"I want to make it to Santiago tonight," I said.

"You mean run all the way and not sleep?" she asked.

"Yes."

"All right, I'll do it with you," she said, enjoying the challenge.

We began to run faster. We ran for fifteen kilometers (more than nine miles), keeping a steady pace as we talked about what she and her husband had learned from the Camino about themselves.

"We walked apart for a month and communicated through messages at the *refugios*. We've decided to stay together."

"That's so romantic," I said.

"No," she answered. "We finally got real with each other."

"Yeah," I said, "reality is a good thing."

Consuelo laughed. I wondered what *her* dream-visions had been like.

It began to rain. We took a wrong turn. Then another. I had my Gortex jacket around my waist. I put it on. Consuelo stopped to pee. I kept running. There was a car up ahead, lying in wait. Consuelo caught up to me. We ran toward the car. It was José. Ali and Carlos were in the car too. We jumped in and drove for a while until we found the next arrow. Then we all got out and ran on the main highway, until Carlos said he thought we should take the small Camino path. We agreed. But soon we ran into a barrage of TV cameras. Consuelo ran in front of me, holding out her hand to cover my face from the lenses. She looked like a protective red bat because of her outstretched red poncho.

We began to sing. "I Want to Hold Your Hand" interspersed with "Ave Maria." Ali couldn't keep up. Carlos stayed with her. I knew I would outrun Ali, and I knew this time that I wouldn't see her again. So I slowed down and reached into my money bag around my waist and pulled out *pesetas* for her to give to José. "It's too much," she argued, stumbling to keep up. "I will tip him too." Breathlessly, we talked about what was fair, because if I didn't see him again and because he had my backpack, I wanted him to mail me my precious tapes. She said she would see to that. Finally, I just stuffed a wad of money in her hand, blew her a kiss, yelled *"Ultreya,"* and broke into a trot. The TV reporters couldn't keep up because their cameras were too heavy.

Carlos remained with Ali. I looked back to etch them in my memory. It would turn out that Carlos had been right. I never saw either of them again.

✢ ✢ ✢

Consuelo and I ran past the Mount of Joy until we reached the sign on the road that said Santiago de Compostela. There were hundreds of TV cameras there. I raised my staff into the air and with the rain pouring into my face, I sang "Santiago, Here I Come" to the tune of "California, Here I Come." Consuelo joined in with harmony. *That* picture they got; along with musical accompaniment.

We outran the press for another ten kilometers (about six and one half miles) until we reached some stone steps. We skipped down the steps and saw a car swoop around the corner and stop in front of us. Anna was inside. She yelled, "Get in, there are hundreds of reporters up ahead. You have crossed the city line on foot. That's all that matters. You made it. Now you must go to the cathedral without the press."

Consuelo and I stuffed ourselves and our staffs into the car and sped away toward the church across the city, where we would pay our respects to Saint James—Santiago de Compostela—the saint with no head. I felt the same way.

By then the press didn't know where I was or whom I was walking with. Ali, Juan, Carlos, the Irish girls, the Germans, the man in the wheelchair, or a pack of dogs? No, I was in a car with a red flying bat from Brazil.

✢ ✢ ✢

And at last, we reached the magnificent cathedral in Compostela and climbed the stone stairway. Begun in the ninth century, it is an architectural marvel, a masterpiece that houses the tomb of Saint James beneath its high altar.

We were greeted by a priest who led us to the statue of the saint that crowns the altar. As was customary, I climbed the stairs, which were behind the statue, and stood there looking up at the back of its head. Anna took a picture of me hugging the statue. I gave Saint James my thanks for being an inspiration to do this journey. I climbed down and went to have my *carné* stamped, the final stamp to prove I had completed the Camino. The priest said the man who stamped *carnés* would not return until tomorrow. Anna begged him in her most eloquent Spanish. I looked on. He didn't know who I was or why I was in such a hurry. Finally, he said *he* would sign it, since he made up the *carnés* himself.

A few press wandered into the cathedral, but out of respect took no pictures. The priest sensed something and looked out the window. There were cameras and reporters swarming everywhere. He looked at me quizzically but said nothing. Then Anna told him who I was and of my quest to leave Santiago unaccosted. He nodded, and then as he gave me a required dissertation on the symbolism of the pilgrimage and as he bathed my feet at my completion, he peppered me with questions about Hollywood.

✳   ✳   ✳

At the completion of my foot bathing, I asked if there was a secret exit from the church. I knew the longer I stayed, the more the press would disturb everyone else's spiritual completion.

The priest was confused as to how to handle me. I asked if I could use the telephone. He said yes. I called the airport and made a reservation for a flight to Madrid at nine-thirty. It was now eight o'clock. I didn't know where José was. He had my backpack with all my notes and tapes; but my credit cards, money, passport, and gold cross were around my waist. I would just trust that Ali would handle José.

I rushed to every window and looked out. There were photographers and reporters at every entrance to the church.

Finally, I found an exit way in the back where there was only one camera crew. Anna's car was there with a driver!

I hurriedly said thank you to the priest, clutched my stamped *carné,* hugged Consuelo and Anna. Anna said she would meet me in Madrid. I waved good-bye and streaked out the door and into Anna's car, leaving all of them behind. The TV camera crew didn't even notice.

I felt a personal triumph.

The driver and I sped toward the airport. I looked in the rearview mirror. There was José in his car alone. He drove up beside my car, rolled down his window, and handed me my backpack. I yelled thank you and handed him my water bottle and new blue hat as a memento of thanks. He smiled. I knew Ali would give him my big tip.

I and my staff headed toward the airport. I felt no sentimentality over what I had been through or accomplished. I would think about that later.

I had walked 780 kilometers—nearly 500 miles. It was July 3. I got my independence the day before I was supposed to. I wondered one thing—had I walked past my bench?

Epilogue
The Journey Continues

As I boarded the plane, I looked and felt like a refugee, a refugee from another time.

I carried my trusty staff over my head. The stewardess quickly commandeered it and stowed it in the back of the plane.

The other passengers looked at my sweaty, two-toned hair, my sunburned, mottled face, filthy boots, tattered leggings, and dilapidated backpack, which now contained only my tapes, my guidebook, my sleeping bag, and a pair of thong shoes. They tried to be discreet, but the passenger I crawled over and sat down next to was not pleased. I wished I had some perfume.

I sat back in the seat trying to be inconspicuous.

The plane took off, and I breathed a contented sigh of accomplishment. Now what would I do with it?

I looked down through the summer twilight.

Beyond Compostela, I saw Finisterre dropping off into the Atlantic. Before my eyes scrolled the pictures I had seen of a once magnificent continent that brought about its own destruction. Yes, I thought, I had walked the Camino in order to understand what we were capable of as human beings—such spiritual magnificence and such destructive fragmentation of our own souls. Were we repeating such dramas even today because we hadn't remembered what we came from?

In a state of reflection and reverie, I looked down at my beloved Camino, threading its way through the cool Spanish hills and valleys and the mesetas of searing, stillborn, shimmering heat. Were other pilgrims having internal journeys of their own so mind-altering that they also couldn't speak of them to others?

Would the *refugios* be places of retreat and safe haven because of what the pilgrims might be experiencing within themselves?

I peered out of the window, soaring above the barking dogs who tested fear; the snarling, packlike press who tested truth and anger; the kind country people who appreciated true *ultreya;* the churches of timeless opulence and spiritual obedience; and more than anything else, the life-sustaining water fountains that made the Camino possible.

Where were Ali and Carlos now? Would they soon be arguing over the true meaning of Saint James? Had the Irish girls
carried their hot plate and sausages to the end? Would Juan be
chastised by the press for failing to get them a story? Did José
feel pride for helping me elude them? Would the man in the
wheelchair career into the magnificent cathedral in Compostela
at seventy miles an hour with divine guidance helping him up
the stone steps? Was Baby Consuelo singing at the feet of the
saint? Would the German man arrive drunk? Was Javier still trying to crawl into someone's bunk? And were the priests still
handing out sturdy staffs to pilgrims in the hope of soliciting
donations?

Looking down at the landscape below, I imagined that I
could see Charlemagne and his armies, the Moors and their
conflicts, the individual stories of our lives and events. I was the
Moorish lassie, dark hair flying in the wind as I rode my horse
and sputtering obscenities in a cold stream after having been
baptized. And over all of it hovered John the Scot, the cleric-
teacher, somehow still narrating in my head: "Remember who
you are and what you have been."

Then I turned in my seat and once again looked behind
me, across the face of the country I had just traversed. Had it
truly connected to a once magnificent continent, an unknown
world that had sunk long ago? And had that continent been a
colony of a yet more ancient spiritual civilization that had been
the beginning of what humankind was intended to be?

Yes, I had walked toward those unknown worlds, looking for who I was and who I had been then.

I imagined that I saw those momentous events: the unknown worlds sinking beneath the waves. I thought about our known world today. Would history repeat itself? Would we go under because we hadn't acknowledged the lessons of the past? We didn't seem to understand our fundamental soul connection to the Great God-Goddess Spirit, the first word, the origin of ALL.

Then I wondered: Was what we called imagination truly based on soul memory? Would we ever know the truth of our soul's past and therefore dream a more magnificent future? Would we learn to trust that once, billions of years ago, the Divine Spirit had been lonely and created us into being, to live as a family of children who loved the Deity with all our hearts and all our souls and our neighbor as ourselves?

I pulled out my gold cross and held it tightly. Yes, I could imagine such a thing.

*   *   *

Anna arrived in Madrid the day after I did. I slept for two days and found that walking was more painful without the energy of the Camino. I shopped for a new leather purse and ate desserts. I couldn't share my experience with Anna. It was too soon. I have communicated with her since the trek and explained that

I needed to write what had happened to me rather than talk it. We are deep friends, and when we parted and she went back to Brazil, I knew my journey was, as she had predicted, "just the beginning."

When I left Spain, I went directly to Kathleen in London. I did share some of my experiences and revelations with her, but in her condition she had enough to cope with. "I'm ready for a soul revelation now myself," she said sadly. She thanked me for doing the trek, in part, for her. She loved hearing about the hills and *mesetas* and flourishing waterfalls and diverse pilgrims and the dogs, and even the press. Where Lemuria and Atlantis were concerned, she thought I had a creative and magnificent imagination. When I asked her to define imagination, she fell asleep. I could understand really.

I stayed with her for a week. She talked for many hours about her life, her past relationships and what she had done and not done with them.

She was creative herself and an intellectual who had an open mind and a full heart and a need to understand who she was.

During the days in London, I felt compelled to continue walking all over the parks and city. I felt naked without my backpack, which I wore regardless of my wardrobe.

I said good-bye to Kathleen, knowing that I probably would not see her again.

And when she died, some months later, the loss of her friendship marked the beginning of my contemplation upon how I would tell the tale of our combined struggle to under-stand who we were in relation to others, to time, to history, and why we wondered so deeply about it.

Her royal dignity, her generosity of spirit, and her fragile beauty and authentic glamour will remain with me always. She was a woman intrigued with the real meaning of intelligence and the loss of paradise, who went on to find her own.

Although Ali and Carlos and I exchanged addresses, I've had no further contact with them. It is as though our experi-ences together stand isolated in time, precious and unvisitable again.

I have also not had contact with the person who wrote me the insistent anonymous letters that so influenced me to do the Camino. I have no idea whom or where those letters came from.

My great regret is that I have no personal photographs, but then mere one-dimensional pictures wouldn't do justice to the experience anyway. The only existing photographs were taken by the press.

Can I prove that Lemuria and Atlantis existed? Of course not. But if I can "imagine" them in such detail, then where does that come from? The recesses of my ancient creative memories? Of one thing I am sure—I have a soul, and it knows more than I can presently comprehend with my mind.

I have no doubt that I have lived before and will live again. Too much synchronicity between certain relationships I've had with people proves that to me *and* many of those people.

Did such an event as sexual division occur eons ago? Myths are not isolated notions, particularly when they occur in many cultures. If we consider ourselves genetic engineers today through DNA and cloning, why couldn't we have done the same in an advanced society long ago? The absence of evidence does not mean the evidence of absence. I think human beings have always enjoyed toying with playing God, since that creational energy exists in all of us.

Perhaps such an event does lie behind the longing so many have to find the other half of themselves in another. Perhaps it also informs the battles and misunderstandings between male and female today.

And does the role of extraterrestrial input enter into the evaluation of who we are as humans?

I think it is foolish to believe we are alone in the cosmic scheme of life in the vast universe. And there is much evidence that they might have visited and *are* visiting earth.

Therefore, I believe it is time for light to shine on possible cover-ups and for us to open ourselves to new horizons by acknowledging the full potential of their existence.

The earth energy itself holds the unexplained mysteries of our spiritual origins. As I walked our planet's beloved surface, I realized deeply how important it is to protect her. The earth mother is our link to who we are as her spiritual children. And as her inhabitants, our balance and harmony will ensure hers. If nature follows consciousness, then it is up to us to keep ourselves harmonious so that the earth will reflect just that. And what is time? Is it so flexible that one can experience everything at once?

It is said that the Buddha closed his eyes for only a few moments and lived ninety-nine thousand incarnations. This sense of God was so profound he could bend time.

Was my experience only expanded awareness brought on by the energy of the Camino?

Would I enhance my knowledge by acknowledging that all of my soul's experience is recorded in its memory?

And imagination? Who are any of us in terms of what we perceive to be real? Each of us is his or her own creation. That is the miracle of the artscape of humanity. Perhaps we have each experienced "good" and "evil" and each lifetime provides us with the lessons of life as we journey back toward the Divine Deity. A person's most profound insights are often regarded as socially unacceptable and even delusional. Should we become "certain" of them because less than that would not be worthy of God?

Perhaps all of it is simple. We came from the Divine; we create with that imaginative energy until we return to it. Lifetime after lifetime.

And John the Scot?

Dear Reader, he comes to me from time to time. He was with me during the writing of this tale, as was the energy of the gold cross, which I wear always. I consider John my good friend and teacher because he taught me that to discount him or anything I "learned" would be to renounce my own talent for creativity.

We each create it all. And again, the absence of evidence does not mean the evidence of absence.

Imagine that.